Simple Snack Cakes

100 RECIPES FOR
SWEET & SAVORY SNACKABLE CAKES

Jennifer Lee

ROCK POINT

This edition published in 2026 by Rock Point,
an imprint of The Quarto Group,
135 West 36th Street, 13th Floor,
New York, NY 10018, USA
(212) 779-4972
www.Quarto.com

Contains content originally published in 2014 as *5-Minute Mug Cakes* by Race Point Publishing, an imprint of The Quarto Group, 142 West 36th Street, 4th Floor, New York, NY 10018, USA.

EEA Representation, WTS Tax d.o.o.,
Žanova ulica 3, 4000 Kranj, Slovenia.
www.wts-tax.si

Rock Point titles are also available at discount for retail, wholesale, promotional, and bulk purchase. For details, contact the Special Sales Manager by email at specialsales@quarto.com or by mail at The Quarto Group, Attn: Special Sales Manager, 100 Cummings Center, Suite 265D
Beverly, MA 01915 USA.

10 9 8 7 6 5 4 3 2 1

ISBN: 978-1-57715-573-7

Digital edition published in 2026
eISBN: 978-1-57715-635-2

Library of Congress Control Number: 2025942957

Group Publisher: Rage Kindelsperger
Editorial Director: Erin Canning
Creative Director: Laura Drew
Managing Editor: Cara Donaldson
Editor: Kristy Mucci
Cover and Interior Design: Tara Long
Food Photography and Food Styling: Jen Straus on cover and pages 3, 7, 22, 24, 30, 34, 44, 48, 50, 58, 60, 64, 68, 70, 76, 90, 92, 100, 104, 108, 112, 118, 122, 126, 130, 150, 156, 160, 164, 176, 178
Food Photography: Jon Meade on pages 114, 154
Food Styling: Michelle Lo on pages 114, 154
Photo courtesy Jennifer Lee page 172

Printed in Huizhou City, Guangdong, China
TT122025

TO GRAYSON,

my inspiration for writing this book

Contents

Introduction

Looking for a simple, quick, and easy cake to make? You've come to the right place. This book shares 100 simple snack cake recipes, including indulgent cakes, healthy cakes, and savory cakes, so there is something for everyone.

What Are Snack Cakes?

Snack cakes are cakes made for casual snacking. They are usually made with just a handful of ingredients, don't require a lot of time to make, and often don't require any special equipment. Most recipes in this book can be prepared in less than five minutes and can be cooked in the microwave, oven, or air fryer. These recipes are perfect for those days when you just need a quick, scrumptious snack that requires little effort and few ingredients.

The recipes in this book are also designed for small servings—perfect for one or two or just a few people. They can also be doubled if you need to feed a larger group.

Many of the treats in this book are brand-new, never before published recipes. There are much-loved classics like Vanilla cake (page 107), Classic Chocolate cake (page 24), and Afternoon Tea cake (page 36). For the kid at heart or the kid in your home, you'll find nostalgic concoctions like the Hostess (Cup)cake (page 92), S'mores cake (page 103), Peanut Butter & Jelly cake (page 102), and Hot Cocoa cake (page 98), as well as adorable holiday-themed recipes with festive flavors like pumpkin, gingerbread, eggnog, and even Halloween candy! I've also transformed sweet breakfast favorites into mug cake form—try the decadent Giant Pancake (page 74) or French Toast cake (page 75), the Blueberry Muffin Streusel (page 73) or the Honey Swirl cake (page 79). There are even savory cakes like Pizza Bundt cake (page 170) and Bacon Bread (page 171) for those moments when you don't crave something sweet!

For people with dietary restrictions, I've created healthy cakes that don't contain wheat flour, refined sugar, or dairy. And finally, for the optimal instant-cake experience, you'll find recipes requiring only four ingredients or less—no special trip to the supermarket necessary! Each recipe has been tested, re-tested, and tested again, to ensure that only the best ended up in this book.

Perhaps you're too busy or too exhausted to make a fancy layer cake. Or you're baking with young kids and you need something simple and easy to suit their short attention spans. Maybe it's late at night and you have a sudden, unrelenting craving for a slice of cake, yet there are no baked goods within reach. You might be cramming for a test or working on a big project, and you just really need an instant pick-me-up. Or maybe you've suffered the cruel misfortune of a broken-down oven. Whatever the circumstances, these cake recipes offer a quick and satisfying solution: With minimal prep and cleanup, they are great for virtually any situation, whether you're a baking novice or a magician in the kitchen, and whether you're snacking solo or serving guests. I hope you have a great time trying out these easy recipes, and I hope you reach for this book whenever the cake mood strikes.

Snack Cake Essentials

Tips for Success

Here are a few tips to keep in mind for successful snack cakes:

- Try your best to follow the recipe exactly as written. Most of the recipes in this book require very few ingredients. As a result, even slight changes to amounts or an ingredient substitution can cause the recipe to not turn out properly.
- Measure the ingredients correctly. Precision is key when you're working with fewer ingredients. Before starting any recipe, I highly encourage you to read through the Main Ingredients section (page 10). There I discuss in detail the most used ingredients for my recipes and how to properly measure them.
- Cooking times can vary. The recipes in this book provide an estimated cooking time but don't rely so heavily on the time given. There are a lot of factors that can affect cooking time, including but not limited to:
    - Ovens, microwaves, and air fryers can run hotter or colder to varying degrees.
    - The thickness or material of a baking dish or pan can affect how quickly it heats up and cooks the cake.
    - The size of a baking dish or pan can also affect how thick your batter is and how long it will take to cook. If you use something larger or smaller than what's called for in the recipe, you'll have to adjust your baking time accordingly.
    - Your ingredients: Different brands may contain more fat, more liquid, more sugar, all which can affect baking time.

- The temperature and humidity levels in your kitchen can also affect ingredients and cooking time.
- The freshness of your baking powder: Baking powder has a very short shelf life and needs to be replaced every few months. If your cake is not rising properly, it may be that your baking powder isn't fresh enough.

- Bake in the middle of the oven and don't overcrowd it. The ideal spot to bake a cake is in the middle of the oven with nothing else above or below it. This allows for a more even heat distribution. If you place a cake too close to the top of the oven, you risk the top burning before the cake is done. If it's too close to the bottom, the bottom might overcook before the rest of the cake is done. I also recommend not adding other things to the oven at the same time because this can also affect the heat distribution.
- Keep the oven door closed. When you open the oven door, you let out heat, which will change the temperature inside the oven. This can cause your cake to deflate or bake unevenly.

Main Ingredients

Here are some of the most-used ingredients you'll need for the recipes in this book.

Flours

ALL-PURPOSE FLOUR

When a recipe in this book calls for all-purpose flour, I am referring to wheat flour with 3 grams of protein per ¼ cup (30 g). Flour can vary in protein levels, especially in different countries. Even within the United States, where all-purpose flour generally contains ten percent protein, there are some brands of all-purpose flour that contain more (such as King Arthur and Bob's Red Mill brands). How much protein is in flour greatly affects a recipe because protein absorbs moisture. If you were to use a high-protein all-purpose flour instead of a standard all-purpose flour, it could result in your cakes being too dry and crumbly. Similarly, if you use a low-protein flour in place of all-purpose flour, your batter may be too liquid, resulting in a gummy texture.

CAKE FLOUR

Cake flour is a lower-protein flour and produces a more delicate crumb. There are a few cakes in this book that require cake flour. Make sure your cake flour has 2 grams of protein per ¼ cup (28 g).

HOW TO MEASURE FLOUR

To properly measure flour for the recipes in this book, first fluff up the flour with a spoon. Then spoon the flour into your measuring spoon or cup, then level it off with the back of a knife. You do not want to directly scoop the flour from the bag into your measuring cup—this results in too much flour and will make your cakes dry and tough.

Baking Powder

The majority of these recipes calls for baking powder. Be sure not to confuse or substitute it with baking soda. Both baking powder and baking soda are leavening agents, producing carbon dioxide, which allows the baked goods to rise, but they are not interchangeable. Baking soda is sodium bicarbonate: It needs an acidic ingredient to interact with before it releases carbon dioxide (and it is four times as strong as baking powder).

Baking powder is part sodium bicarbonate, already mixed with an acidic element and a starch. Using baking powder and baking soda will also yield different textures, so always use what the recipe calls for.

Make sure your baking powder is fresh. Baking powder needs to be replaced every few months or else it loses its effectiveness. I replace my baking powder every three to four months. If you haven't baked in a while, and your cake just isn't rising, it's likely that your baking powder is old.

ALUMINUM-FREE BAKING POWDER

For recipes that use a large amount of baking powder, I always recommend using aluminum-free baking powder to eliminate any potential metallic aftertaste. I like using Whole Foods 365 Aluminum-Free Baking Powder.

Baking Soda

A few recipes in this book use baking soda or a combination of baking soda and powder. Make sure your baking soda is fresh, as it also has a short shelf-life, like baking powder. Also make sure you don't omit the acidic ingredient in a cake.

Sugar

In addition to being a sweetener, sugar also alters the moisture, texture, and structure of a cake. As a result, it is important to not substitute another sweetener for sugar. Doing so can cause the cake to be dry, crumbly, dense, or to not rise properly.

GRANULATED SUGAR

Recipes in this book call for granulated sugar. This is the most common sugar found in people's pantries and used for cooking—often referred to as regular sugar, white sugar, or table sugar.

BROWN SUGAR

Brown sugar is granulated sugar with molasses. Light brown sugar has a golden color and less molasses flavor. Dark brown sugar has a darker brown hue and a richer molasses flavor. Most of the recipes in this book that use brown sugar call for light brown sugar. While the recipes work better with light brown sugar, you can substitute dark brown if that's all you have on hand. A few recipes specify dark brown sugar to obtain a deeper molasses flavor.

Note: Brown sugar will harden if it is not stored in a tightly sealed container. If that happens, you can heat it up in the microwave for a few seconds to make it moist again.

HOW TO MEASURE BROWN SUGAR

Unlike flour, you do want brown sugar to be packed when you measure it (unless the recipe specifies not to). To do so, scoop your measuring cup or spoon directly into the brown sugar bag, scooping up a little more than the measuring cup or spoon can hold. Then use your fingers to pack it down, and level off with a knife if needed. When you turn out the brown sugar, it should hold the shape of the cup or spoon.

CONFECTIONERS' SUGAR

Confectioners' sugar (also called powdered sugar) is granulated sugar that has been ground to a smooth powder. It is usually mixed with cornstarch to prevent caking. It's often used to make frostings because it dissolves more easily. Make sure to use a good-quality brand of confectioners' sugar. Some cheaper brands will often add too much cornstarch as filler, which can result in a bad aftertaste.

Milk

Most of the recipes in this book call for fat-free milk to make the cakes healthier. You can substitute with low-fat. However, if a recipe specifies whole milk, do not try to substitute low-fat or fat-free milk, as the cake needs the fat from the whole milk.

Vanilla

Vanilla adds flavor and depth to cake as well as enhancing the sweetness; I don't recommend leaving it out if a cake calls for it. When a recipe calls for vanilla, I am referring to pure vanilla extract. Be sure to avoid imitation vanilla, which can leave an artificial aftertaste.

Canola or Avocado Oil

Most of the cakes in this book use canola or avocado oil because of their neutral flavors. Avoid using olive oil and any other oils that have a distinct flavor, as they will alter the taste of the cakes. Also avoid using melted butter instead of oil. Butter has less fat content than oil, so a direct substitution will lead to a dryer cake.

Butter

For recipes that require butter, always use unsalted butter. Unsalted butter is generally used in baking because it gives you control of the salt content that goes into the dessert.

Eggs

In general, I don't like using eggs in my single-serving cakes because using a whole egg can make a cake taste eggy or give it a rubbery or gummy texture. There are a few recipes in this book in which the texture simply wouldn't be right without some egg in the batter. When a recipe calls for a large egg, I am referring to a standard US large egg, which weighs about 2 ounces (57 g) and yields about 3¼ tablespoons (46 ml) in volume. Egg sizes can differ in different countries so, if possible, you will want to weigh your eggs to make sure you are adding the correct amount to the recipe.

Chocolate

SEMISWEET CHOCOLATE

Most of the recipes use semisweet chocolate chips. You don't have to use standard chocolate chips. You can use any other form of semisweet chocolate, like semisweet baking chocolate bars (chopped), semisweet chocolate discs, or semisweet chocolate chunks. But please stick to using semisweet chocolate, otherwise, the taste and texture of the cake will be affected. Also, please note that if you are using something other than standard-size chocolate chips, you should weigh the chocolate to make sure you get the right amount.

A NOTE ON MELTING CHOCOLATE

Be careful when melting the chips in the microwave—you don't want to overheat and burn the chocolate. I was able to heat my chocolate with cold milk at full power without any issues, but if you find your microwave is too strong, you can reduce the power level.

UNSWEETENED COCOA POWDER

All the recipes that call for unsweetened cocoa powder in this book require Dutch-process cocoa powder. There are two types of unsweetened cocoa powder: Dutch-process and natural. Dutch-process, or alkalized, cocoa powder has been treated with an alkalizing agent to reduce the acidity of the cocoa. It's usually darker in color and yields a richer cocoa flavor and has a less-bitter taste. Look for "Dutch process" or "processed with alkali" on the label. In the United States, most unsweetened cocoa powder sold at supermarkets is natural cocoa powder. In Europe, Dutch-process is more common. If you are in the US, you can find Dutch-process cocoa powder in baking stores and through online merchants like Amazon.

Natural cocoa tends to be more bitter and will often be labeled "natural unsweetened" or have no label at all. This is usually the unsweetened cocoa found at supermarkets. Natural cocoa is more acidic and leaves a bitter taste, which is why it's not used as often in baked goods—except for recipes calling for baking soda (as discussed earlier, baking soda needs an acidic element to react with). If a recipe specifies natural cocoa, you cannot substitute it for Dutch-processed because the recipe is depending on the acidity of the natural cocoa.

And finally, make sure you don't mistake unsweetened cocoa powder for the sweetened cocoa powder used to make hot chocolate. (The one recipe in this book that does use sweetened cocoa powder is the Hot Cocoa cake on page 98, as stated in the ingredients).

Peanut Butter

The recipes in this book were tested with regular sweetened peanut butter. Unless a recipe specifically calls for natural peanut butter (the kind with no added oils), I don't recommend using it, as it can affect the outcome of the cake. For example, in the Flourless Peanut Butter cake (page 160), using natural peanut butter will result in the sugar remaining crunchy because the cake needs the added oils to melt the sugar.

Nonstick Cooking Spray

Many of the recipes require you to grease your bakeware with nonstick cooking spray. This doesn't affect the cake itself, but it does help to ensure that your cake doesn't stick to the pan and can be removed easily. You will want to use a neutral nonstick cooking spray like a canola or avocado oil spray. If you prefer to not use nonstick cooking spray, you can omit it, but make sure your baking pan is lined with parchment paper to prevent sticking.

Some of the recipes require nonstick cooking spray and parchment paper. In this case, the cooking spray is mainly used to help the parchment paper stick so that it doesn't cause indents in your finished snack cake.

The one exception for greasing is for the microwave mug cakes. Since mug cakes are designed specifically to be eaten in the mug, you don't need to release it. Also, when the mug cake is cooked in the microwave, the cooking process is much faster, and it is more like steaming than baking. As a result, the cake doesn't stick as much.

Kitchen Equipment

The majority of these recipes are designed for either a microwave, oven, or air fryer. In addition, you'll need some heat-safe dishes and baking pans.

Microwave

The cooking times given for the recipes in this book are based on the 1100-watt microwave in my kitchen, completed at the full power setting. Microwaves differ in wattage, so you may have to make some time adjustments or reduce the power setting. The material of your mug can also affect cooking time.

Most of the microwave cakes will take about one minute to cook. If you need to adjust the cooking time, make sure to add or subtract only about fifteen seconds at a time. You want to be very careful not to overcook the cake. Once overcooked, it becomes hard, dry, or rubbery—and even a mere fifteen seconds can make a huge difference. It is much better to undercook the cake than to overcook it, since the cake will continue to cook in the mug once you've removed it from the microwave to cool.

Oven

The recipes in this book are designed for a standard conventional oven. Bake these snack cakes on the middle rack, ideally right in the center and without other items next to, above, or below, as that can make the heat distribution uneven.

These recipes have not been tested with a convection oven. Convection ovens have a fan that helps circulate hot air. As a result, recipes will often cook faster and may need a lower temperature, or a cake may dry out before it's finished cooking. If you have a convection oven, I recommend turning off the convection setting for these recipes.

Air Fryer

The recipes in this book were tested in a basket-style air fryer. Depending on your air fryer, you may need to adjust the temperature and/or time for the recipe.

Baking Pans

ROUND CAKE PAN

The majority of the larger cakes in this book require a 6-inch (15 cm) round baking pan. This size will fit into most air fryers. There are a few cakes that use a 7-inch (17 cm) round cake pan; these were recipes where the ingredient amounts just didn't work well for anything smaller.

LOAF PAN

Most of the loaf pan recipes in this book use a 3 by 7-inch (7.5 by 17 cm) loaf pan, though a few use a 4 by 8-inch (10 by 20 cm) loaf pan. If you don't have a 3 by 7-inch (7.5 by 17 cm) loaf pan, you can split the batter into smaller loaf pans for air fryer recipes. Or if your air fryer can fit a 4 by 8-inch (10 by 20 cm) loaf pan, you can use one, but your loaf won't bake as high.

OVERSIZED MUG

I recommend using a microwave-safe mug that can hold at least 12 ounces (360 ml) of liquid. I usually use mugs that hold between 12 and 16 ounces (360 and 480 ml). A large mug is required to ensure that the batter stays in the mug when it is cooking and rising. You don't want it to overflow and make a mess in your microwave.

While your favorite oversized mug will likely work just fine, I've cooked with enough different mugs to be able to offer a few pointers for finding the optimal kind.

The ideal mug will be tall, curved, with thick walls.

- **Why tall?** The height ensures that your cake does not overflow.
- **Why curved?** Curved walls allow you to thoroughly mix your ingredients without anything getting stuck in crevices at the bottom of the mug. When the interior is completely straight, flour is more likely to wedge itself into the corners. If you have no choice but to cook with a straight mug, be sure to maneuver your whisk around to get all the flour that may be stuck in the inner bottom ring.
- **Why thick?** Thick walls withstand heat better than thin ones. Mugs made of thin material sometimes overheat quickly, which can overcook or unevenly cook your cake.

Once the cake is done cooking, you can plate it in a smaller mug for a prettier presentation.

If you want to achieve the overflowing appearance you see in the photos, my suggestion is to first make the recipe in an oversized mug. Once you have an idea how high that specific cake will rise, you can start testing it in smaller mugs until you find the ideal one—where the cake will rise past the rim without the batter dripping everywhere in your microwave.

Ramekins

For the single-serving cakes in this book, I recommend making them in an 8-ounce (240 ml) microwave- and oven-safe ramekin. This size should be big enough for the cake to rise and expand without overflowing. You may be able to use a 7-ounce (210 ml) or 6-ounce (180 ml) ramekin if that is all you have, but the cake will rise above the ramekin as it cooks and there is a chance the batter will overflow.

Measuring Cups

If you plan on using measuring cups instead of a scale for these recipes, please try to use measuring cups that are very accurate to keep your cakes from turning out too dry or too wet.

Measuring spoons

You'll need a set of measuring spoons to measure many of the ingredients for these recipes. Measuring spoons will vary in accuracy. Use a set you know to be very accurate and try to use the same set to measure the ingredients in the entire recipe, even though this may mean you need to wash a spoon or two in between.

For dry ingredients, make sure to level off the measuring spoon after scooping an ingredient so you have the right amount. If you are working with sticky ingredients like a Nutella spread or honey, try to scrape the sides of the measuring spoon to get it all into the mixing bowl.

Silicone Spatula

Many recipes require a spatula. I prefer using silicone spatulas because they are heatproof. When a recipe calls for mixing with a spatula it is usually to prevent overworking your cake batter.

Whisks

The mug-cake recipes in this book require a mini whisk to mix the batter. It should easily mix ingredients in the narrow confines of a mug—a standard whisk will be too big. Mini whisks cost only a few dollars and can be found in the baking aisle of grocery stores, specialty baking shops, and through online merchants like Amazon.

For the larger cakes in this book, I recommend a medium-size regular whisk. You can use a large whisk, but I find it isn't necessary because you aren't working with that much batter. I prefer using a medium whisk because it's more compact and the wire loops are closer together, which helps mix out lumps from the cake batter.

Parchment Paper

Many recipes call for the pan to be lined with parchment paper. Parchment paper creates a nonstick surface so the cake can easily be removed. Be sure to use a high-quality brand of parchment paper (I like using Reynolds brand).

Chocolate Snack Cakes

This is not a complete list of all the chocolate recipes in this book because a few of them fit better into other chapters, but here you'll find some of my most decadent and mouthwatering chocolate-based cake recipes, including Chocolate Lava (page 26), Cookies & Cream (page 28), and Salted-Caramel Chocolate (page 33).

Classic Chocolate

Don't let the simplicity of this recipe fool you: It has a rich flavor that completely satisfies chocolate cravings.

SERVES 1 OR 2

¼ cup (45 g) semisweet chocolate chips

3 tablespoons fat-free milk

2 tablespoons all-purpose flour

¼ teaspoon baking powder

½ tablespoon canola or avocado oil

Chocolate Ganache Frosting (page 182), for topping, (optional)

Microwave Instructions

1. In an oversized microwave-safe mug, combine the chocolate chips and milk. Microwave for about 40 seconds. Mix with a small whisk until the chocolate is completely melted. Add the flour, baking powder, and oil and whisk until the batter is smooth.
2. Microwave for about 1 minute. If the cake is not done, heat for an additional 15 seconds. Let the cake cool for a few minutes. If using, top with the chocolate ganache frosting. This cake is best consumed while still warm or within a few hours of being cooked.

Oven and Air Fryer Instructions

1. Preheat the oven to 350°F (175°C) or the air fryer to 325°F (160°C).
2. In an oversized microwave-safe mug, combine the chocolate chips and milk. Microwave for about 40 seconds. Mix with a small whisk until the chocolate is completely melted. Add the flour, baking powder, and oil and whisk until the batter is smooth.
3. If the mug is oven safe, bake the cake in it. If not, transfer the batter to a greased 8-ounce (240 ml) oven-safe ramekin or similar sized oven-safe baking dish. If using the oven, bake for 20 to 30 minutes, until a toothpick inserted comes out clean. If using the air-fryer, bake the cake for 8 to 12 minutes, until a toothpick inserted comes out clean. Let the cake cool for a few minutes. If using, top with the chocolate ganache frosting. This cake is best consumed while still warm or within a few hours of being cooked.

* Note

You can change the type of chocolate to suit your personal preference. Dark chocolate will make a richer, more bittersweet cake. Milk chocolate will produce a sweeter cake with less cocoa flavor. I don't recommend using white chocolate, as the cake does need cocoa to set.

Chocolate Lava

Warm chocolate cake with a melted chocolate center—what's not to love? It is no wonder this dessert is so popular and shows up on practically every restaurant menu. With this recipe, there's no need to wait for a fancy dinner to indulge in this timeless classic.

SERVES 1 OR 2

¼ cup (45 g) semisweet chocolate chips

3 tablespoons fat-free milk

2 tablespoons all-purpose flour

¼ teaspoon baking powder

½ tablespoon canola or avocado oil

1 chocolate truffle (such as Lindor)

1 teaspoon confectioners' sugar, for topping (optional)

Microwave Instructions

1. In an oversized microwave-safe mug, combine the chocolate chips and milk. Microwave for about 40 seconds. Mix with a small whisk until the chocolate chips are completely melted. Add the flour, baking powder, and oil and whisk until the batter is smooth. Push the chocolate truffle into the center of the batter, until completely covered.
2. Microwave for about 1 minute. If the cake is not done, heat for an additional 15 seconds. Let the cake cool for a few minutes.
3. If using, dust with the confectioners' sugar. This cake is best consumed while still warm (see Note).

Oven and Air Fryer Instructions

1. Preheat the oven to 350°F (175°C) or the air fryer to 325°F (160°C).
2. In an oversized microwave-safe mug, combine the chocolate chips and milk. Microwave for about 40 seconds. Mix with a small whisk until the chocolate chips are completely melted. Add the flour, baking powder, and oil and whisk until the batter is smooth. Push the chocolate truffle into the center of the batter, until completely covered.
3. If the mug is oven-safe, bake the cake in it. If not, transfer the batter to a greased 8-ounce (240 ml) oven-safe ramekin or similar sized oven-safe baking dish. If using the oven, bake for 20 to 30 minutes, until a toothpick inserted comes out clean. If using the air fryer, bake for 8 to 12 minutes, until a toothpick inserted comes out clean. Let the cake cool for a few minutes.
4. If using, dust with the confectioners' sugar. This cake is best consumed while still warm (see Note).

*Note

This cake is best eaten while still warm but be careful because the melted chocolate center may still be very hot!

Cookies & Cream

This cake has a white chocolate base with Oreo chocolate cookie crumbles and cream studded throughout.

SERVES 1 OR 2

1/4 cup (45 g) white chocolate chips

3 tablespoons whole milk

1/4 cup (30 g) all-purpose flour

1/4 teaspoon baking powder

1/2 tablespoon canola or avocado oil

2 Oreo cookies

Cream Cheese Frosting (page 183), for topping (optional)

1 mini Oreo, for decorating (optional)

Microwave Instructions

1. In an oversized microwave-safe mug, microwave the white chocolate chips and milk for about 40 seconds. Mix with a small whisk until the white chocolate is completely melted. Add the flour, baking powder, and oil and whisk until smooth. Add the Oreo cookies and smash them into small chunks with a fork. Microwave for about 1 minute. If necessary, heat for an additional 15 seconds. Let cool for a few minutes.
2. If using, top with the cream cheese frosting and mini Oreo cookie. This cake is best consumed while still warm or within a few hours of being cooked.

Oven and Air Fryer Instructions

1. Preheat the oven or air fryer to 350°F (175°C).
2. In an oversized microwave-safe mug, microwave the white chocolate chips and milk for about 40 seconds. Mix with a small whisk until the white chocolate is completely melted. Add the flour, baking powder, and oil and whisk until smooth. Add the Oreo cookies and smash them into small chunks with a fork. If the mug is oven-safe, bake the cake in it. If not, transfer the batter to a greased 8-ounce (240 ml) oven-safe ramekin or similar sized baking dish. Bake in the oven for 20 to 30 minutes, or in the air fryer for 10 to 15 minutes, until a toothpick inserted comes out clean. Let cool for a few minutes.
3. If using, top with the cream cheese frosting and mini Oreo cookie. This cake is best consumed while still warm or within a few hours of being cooked.

White Chocolate

Are there any white chocolate lovers out there? Well then, this cake is for you.

SERVES 1 OR 2

1/4 cup (45 g) white chocolate chips

3 tablespoons whole milk

3 tablespoons all-purpose flour

1/4 teaspoon baking powder

1/2 tablespoon canola or avocado oil

Cream Cheese Frosting (page 183), for topping (optional)

Microwave Instructions

1. In an oversized microwave-safe mug, microwave the white chocolate chips and milk for about 40 seconds. Mix with a small whisk until the white chocolate is completely melted. Add the flour, baking powder, and oil and whisk until smooth. Microwave for about 1 minute. If necessary, heat for an additional 15 seconds. Let cool for a few minutes.
2. If using, top with the cream cheese frosting. This cake is best consumed while still warm or within a few hours of being cooked.

Oven and Air Fryer Instructions

1. Preheat the oven to 350°F (175°C) or the air fryer to 325°F (160°C).
2. In an oversized microwave-safe mug, microwave the white chocolate chips and milk for about 40 seconds. Mix with a small whisk until the white chocolate is completely melted. Add the flour, baking powder, and oil and whisk until smooth.
3. If the mug is oven-safe, bake the cake in it. If not, transfer the batter to a greased 8-ounce (240 ml) oven-safe ramekin or similar sized baking dish. Bake in the oven for 20 to 30 minutes, or in the air fryer for 10 to 15 minutes, until a toothpick inserted comes out clean. Let cool for a few minutes.
4. If using, top with the cream cheese frosting. This cake is best consumed while still warm or within a few hours of being cooked.

Chocolate Vanilla Marble

Marble cakes are so lovely to look at, with their mesmerizing swirls. This cake takes a little more time because you need to make two separate batters and then swirl them together. But the end result is as pretty as a picture.

SERVES 1 OR 2

1/4 cup (30 g) all-purpose flour

1/4 teaspoon baking powder

1 tablespoon granulated sugar

3 tablespoons fat-free milk

1 tablespoon canola oil, divided

1/8 teaspoon vanilla extract

1/2 tablespoon unsweetened Dutch-process cocoa powder

Microwave Instructions

1. In an oversized microwave-safe mug, combine the flour, baking powder, sugar, milk, and 1/2 tablespoon of the oil. Mix with a small whisk until the batter is smooth.
2. Transfer 2 tablespoons of the batter to a small bowl, add the vanilla, and whisk to combine.
3. To the mug, add the cocoa powder and the remaining 1/2 tablespoon oil and whisk until smooth. Top with dollops of the vanilla batter and, using a butter knife, draw multiple figure eights into the batter to create a marbled effect.
4. Microwave for about 1 minute. If the cake is not done, heat for an additional 15 seconds. Let the cake cool for a few minutes. This cake is best consumed while still warm or within a few hours of being cooked.

Oven and Air Fryer Instructions

1. Preheat the oven or air fryer to 350°F (175°C).
2. In an oversized oven-safe mug (or a greased 8-ounce/240-ml oven-safe ramekin or similar sized oven-safe baking dish), combine the flour, baking powder, sugar, milk, and 1/2 tablespoon of the oil. Mix with a small whisk until the batter is smooth.
3. Transfer 2 tablespoons of the batter to a small bowl, add the vanilla, and whisk to combine.
4. To the mug or other dish, add the cocoa powder and the remaining 1/2 tablespoon oil and whisk until smooth. Top with dollops of the vanilla batter and, using a butter knife, draw multiple figure eights into the batter to create a marbled effect.
5. If using the oven, bake for 20 to 30 minutes, until a toothpick inserted comes out clean. If using the air fryer, bake for 10 to 15 minutes, until a toothpick inserted comes out clean. Let the cake cool for a few minutes. This cake is best consumed while still warm or within a few hours of being cooked.

Triple Chocolate

This cake is packed with melted dark chocolate, cocoa powder, and chocolate chips. You might need a glass of milk with this one!

SERVES 1 OR 2

¼ cup (33 g) chopped dark chocolate

3 tablespoons fat-free milk

2 tablespoons all-purpose flour

½ tablespoon unsweetened Dutch-process cocoa powder

¼ teaspoon baking powder

1 tablespoon canola or avocado oil

2 tablespoons semisweet chocolate chips

Microwave Instructions

1. In an oversized microwave-safe mug, microwave the chopped dark chocolate and milk for about 40 seconds. Mix with a small whisk until the chocolate is completely melted. Add the flour, cocoa powder, baking powder, and oil and whisk until smooth. Stir in the chocolate chips.
2. Microwave for about 1 minute. If necessary, heat for an additional 15 seconds. Let cool for a few minutes. This cake is best consumed while still warm or within a few hours of being cooked.

Oven and Air Fryer Instructions

1. Preheat the oven to 350°F (175°C) or the air fryer to 325°F (160°C).
2. In an oversized microwave-safe mug, microwave the chopped dark chocolate and milk for about 40 seconds. Mix with a small whisk until the chocolate is completely melted. Add the flour, cocoa powder, baking powder, and oil and whisk until smooth. Stir in the chocolate chips.
3. If the mug is oven-safe, bake the cake in it. If not, transfer the batter to a greased 8-ounce (240 ml) oven-safe ramekin or similar sized oven-safe baking dish. Bake in the oven for 20 to 30 minutes, or in the air fryer for 8 to 12 minutes, until a toothpick inserted comes out clean. Let cool for a few minutes. This cake is best consumed while still warm or within a few hours of being cooked.

Salted–Caramel Chocolate

Salted caramel heightens the sweetness and richness of chocolate, adding an extra bit of bliss to each bite.

SERVES 1 OR 2

- 1/4 cup (45 g) semisweet chocolate chips
- 3 tablespoons fat-free milk
- 2 tablespoons all-purpose flour
- 1/4 teaspoon baking powder
- 1/2 tablespoon canola or avocado oil
- 2 salted caramels
- Caramel syrup, for drizzling (optional)
- 1 caramel, chopped, for topping (optional)

Microwave Instructions

1. In an oversized microwave-safe mug, microwave the chocolate chips and milk for about 40 seconds. Mix with a small whisk until the chocolate is completely melted. Add the flour, baking powder, and oil and whisk until smooth. Push the caramels into the center of the batter, until completely covered. Microwave for about 1 minute. If necessary, heat for an additional 15 seconds. Let cool for a few minutes.
2. If using, top with the caramel syrup and chopped caramel. This cake is best consumed while still warm or within a few hours of being cooked.

Oven and Air Fryer Instructions

1. Preheat the oven to 350°F (175°C) or the air fryer to 325°F (160°C).
2. In an oversized microwave-safe mug, microwave the chocolate chips and milk for about 40 seconds. Mix with a small whisk until the chocolate is completely melted. Add the flour, baking powder, and oil and whisk until smooth. Push the caramels into the center of the batter, until completely covered. If the mug is oven-safe, bake the cake in it. If not, transfer the batter to a greased 8-ounce (240 ml) oven-safe ramekin or similar sized oven-safe baking dish. Bake in the oven for 20 to 30 minutes, or in the air fryer for 8 to 12 minutes, until a toothpick inserted comes out clean. Let cool for a few minutes.
3. If using, top with the caramel syrup and chopped caramel. This cake is best consumed while still warm or within a few hours of being cooked.

Fruit-Based Snack Cakes

Fruit is especially great to add to baked goods because it adds a natural sweetness and brightens up desserts with vivid colors. Whether you prefer lighter fruit-flavored desserts or you're looking for some ideas to use up leftover fruit this is the chapter for you.

Afternoon Tea

This afternoon tea cake is simple but delicious. It can be topped with nearly any fruit.

Oven and Air Fryer Instructions

1. Preheat the oven or air fryer to 350°F (175°C). Grease a 6-inch (15 cm) round baking pan with nonstick cooking spray and line it with a parchment paper round.
2. In a large bowl, add the flour, baking powder, sugar, egg, vanilla, and oil. Mix vigorously with a whisk until the batter is smooth. Transfer to the prepared baking pan and spread the sliced fruit across the top.
3. If using the oven, bake for about 30 minutes, or until golden on top and a toothpick inserted comes out clean. If using the air fryer, bake for 10 to 15 minutes, until golden on top and a toothpick inserted comes out clean. Let the cake cool for a few minutes.
4. If using, dust with confectioners' sugar. This cake is best consumed while still warm or within a few hours of being cooked.

✱ Note

You can use any fruit you like, and feel free to mix it up with the seasons! Some of my favorites for slicing are apples, pears, and peaches.

SERVES 6 TO 8

½ cup (65 g) all-purpose flour

½ teaspoon baking powder

¼ cup plus 2 tablespoons (75 g) granulated sugar

1 large egg

½ teaspoon vanilla

¼ cup (60 ml) canola or avocado oil

½ cup (70 g) fresh berries or thinly sliced fruit of choice (see Note)

Confectioners' sugar, for topping (optional)

Pumpkin

This pumpkin flavored cake is soft, moist, and fluffy with just the right amount of warm fall spices to round it out. It's one of my favorite fall cakes.

SERVES 6 TO 8

1/4 cup plus 2 tablespoons (85 g) pumpkin puree

1/2 cup (100 g) granulated sugar

2 tablespoons canola or avocado oil

1 cup (125 g) all-purpose flour

1 1/2 teaspoons baking powder

1/4 teaspoon salt

1/2 teaspoon ground cinnamon

Oven and Air Fryer Instructions

1. Preheat the oven or air fryer to 350°F (175°C). Grease a 6-inch (15 cm) round baking pan with nonstick cooking spray and line it with a parchment paper round.
2. In a large bowl, whisk together the pumpkin, sugar, oil, and 1/2 cup (120 ml) of water until smooth. Add the flour, baking powder, salt, and cinnamon; fold in with a spatula until evenly combined.
3. If using the oven, bake for about 35 minutes, or until a toothpick inserted comes out clean. If using the air fryer, bake for 10 to 15 minutes, until a toothpick inserted comes out clean. Let cool completely. Store any leftovers in the fridge or freezer in an airtight container.

Applesauce

This cake is moist, soft, and flavored with the sweetness and tartness of apples.

SERVES 6 TO 8

2/3 cup (165 g) unsweetened applesauce

1/2 cup (100 g) granulated sugar

1 tablespoon unsalted butter, melted

1 cup (125 g) all-purpose flour

1 1/2 teaspoons baking powder

1/4 teaspoon salt

Oven and Air Fryer Instructions

1. Preheat the oven or air fryer to 350°F (175°C). Grease a 6-inch (15 cm) round baking pan with nonstick cooking spray, then line it with parchment paper (leave some overhang for easy removal later).

2. In a large bowl, whisk together the applesauce, sugar, and melted butter until smooth. Add the flour, baking powder, and salt; fold in with a spatula until completely incorporated and there are no clumps. (Make sure to only use a spatula to mix and not a whisk or beater, otherwise you will overmix the batter.) The batter will be thick. Transfer to the prepared baking pan and spread it into an even layer.

3. If using the oven, bake for about 30 minutes, or until a toothpick inserted comes out clean. If using the air fryer, bake for 10 to 15 minutes, until a toothpick inserted comes out clean. Let cool in the pan for 15 minutes.

4. Transfer the cake to a wire rack to cool completely. Store any leftovers in the fridge or freezer in an airtight container.

Strawberries & Cream

One of my favorite summertime treats is strawberries dipped in lightly whipped sweet cream. This recipe starts with a sweet-cream cake base and is studded with bright red berries.

Microwave Instructions

1. In an oversized microwave-safe mug, combine the flour, baking powder, granulated sugar, milk, and cream. Mix with a small whisk until the batter is smooth. Stir in the chopped strawberry.
2. Microwave for about 1 minute. If the cake is not done, heat for an additional 15 seconds. Let the cake cool for a few minutes.
3. If using, top with the whipped cream frosting, sliced strawberry, and confectioners' sugar. This cake is best consumed while still warm or within a few hours of being cooked.

Oven and Air Fryer Instructions

1. Preheat the oven or air fryer to 350°F (175°C).
2. In an oversized oven-safe mug (or a greased 8-ounce/240-ml oven-safe ramekin or similar sized oven-safe baking dish), combine the flour, baking powder, granulated sugar, milk, and cream. Mix with a small whisk until the batter is smooth. Stir in the chopped strawberry.
3. If using the oven, bake for 20 to 30 minutes, until a toothpick inserted comes out clean. If using the air fryer, bake for 10 to 15 minutes, until a toothpick inserted comes out clean. Let the cake cool for a few minutes.
4. If using, top with the whipped cream frosting, sliced strawberry, and confectioners' sugar. This cake is best consumed while still warm or within a few hours of being cooked.

SERVES 1 OR 2

¼ cup (30 g) all-purpose flour

¼ teaspoon baking powder

1½ tablespoons granulated sugar

2 tablespoons fat-free milk

2 tablespoons heavy whipping cream

2 large strawberries, 1 chopped, and 1 sliced, for decorating (optional)

Whipped Cream Frosting (page 183), for topping (optional)

Confectioners' sugar, for topping (optional)

Blueberry

This simple white cake is adorned with the purple-blue splashes of heated blueberries, and a sweet helping of fresh berries..

SERVES 1 OR 2

¼ cup (30 g) all-purpose flour

¼ teaspoon baking powder

2½ teaspoons granulated sugar

3 tablespoons fat-free milk

½ tablespoon canola or avocado oil

¼ teaspoon vanilla extract

10 blueberries, plus 5 for topping (optional; see Note)

Whipped Cream Frosting (page 183), for topping (optional)

Confectioners' sugar, for topping (optional)

✱ Note

You can replace the blueberries with other chopped fresh fruit like strawberries, mangoes, or peaches.

Microwave Instructions

1. In an oversized microwave-safe mug, combine the flour, baking powder, granulated sugar, milk, oil, and vanilla. Mix with a small whisk until the batter is smooth. Stir in 10 blueberries.
2. Microwave for about 1 minute. If the cake is not done, heat for an additional 15 seconds. Let the cake cool for a few minutes.
3. If using, top with the whipped cream frosting, 5 fresh blueberries, and confectioners' sugar. This cake is best consumed while still warm or within a few hours of being cooked.

Oven and Air Fryer Instructions

1. Preheat the oven or air fryer to 350°F (175°C).
2. In an oversized oven-safe mug (or a greased 8-ounce/240-ml oven-safe ramekin or similar sized oven-safe baking dish), combine the flour, baking powder, sugar, milk, oil, and vanilla. Mix with a small whisk until the batter is smooth. Stir in 10 blueberries.
3. If using the oven, bake for 20 to 30 minutes, until a toothpick inserted comes out clean. If using the air fryer, bake for 10 to 15 minutes, until a toothpick inserted comes out clean. Let the cake cool for a few minutes.
4. If using, top with the whipped cream frosting, 5 fresh blueberries, and confectioners' sugar. This cake is best consumed while still warm or within a few hours of being cooked.

Coconut Dream

This cake is a coconut trifecta: coconut milk, coconut flakes, and coconut oil.

SERVES 1 OR 2

¼ cup (30 g) all-purpose flour

¼ teaspoon baking powder

2 teaspoons granulated sugar

2 tablespoons coconut milk

½ tablespoon unrefined coconut oil

1½ tablespoons sweetened coconut flakes, plus 1 tablespoon for topping (optional)

Dairy-Free Whipped Cream Frosting (page 184), for topping (optional)

Microwave Instructions

1. In an oversized microwave-safe mug, combine the flour, baking powder, sugar, coconut milk, coconut oil, and 1 tablespoon of water. Mix with a small whisk until the batter is smooth. Stir in the 1½ tablespoons coconut flakes.
2. Microwave for about 1 minute. If the cake is not done, heat for an additional 15 seconds. Let the cake cool for a few minutes.
3. If using, top with the dairy-free whipped cream frosting and 1 tablespoon sweetened coconut flakes. This cake is best consumed while still warm or within a few hours of being cooked.

Oven and Air Fryer Instructions

1. Preheat the oven or air fryer to 350°F (175°C).
2. In an oversized oven-safe mug (or a greased 8-ounce/240-ml oven-safe ramekin or similar sized oven-safe baking dish), combine the flour, baking powder, sugar, coconut milk, coconut oil, and 1 tablespoon of water. Mix with a small whisk until the batter is smooth. Stir in the 1½ tablespoons coconut flakes.
3. If using the oven, bake for 20 to 30 minutes, until a toothpick inserted comes out clean. If using the air fryer, bake for 10 to 15 minutes, until a toothpick inserted comes out clean. Let the cake cool for a few minutes.
4. If using, top with the dairy-free whipped cream frosting and 1 tablespoon sweetened coconut flakes. This cake is best consumed while still warm or within a few hours of being cooked.

Lemon

This lemon cake is just dreamy. It's moist, lemony, and the perfect balance of sweet and tart.

SERVES 1 OR 2

1/4 cup (30 g) all-purpose flour

1/4 teaspoon baking powder

2 teaspoons granulated sugar

3 tablespoons fat-free milk

1/2 tablespoon canola or avocado oil

1/4 teaspoon vanilla extract

1 teaspoon freshly grated lemon zest, plus 1/2 teaspoon for topping (optional)

1 tablespoon lemon curd

Whipped Cream Frosting (page 183), for topping (optional)

Microwave Instructions

1. In an oversized microwave-safe mug, combine the flour, baking powder, sugar, milk, oil, and vanilla. Mix with a small whisk until the batter is smooth. Add the 1 teaspoon lemon zest and the lemon curd and mix until the batter is smooth.

2. Microwave for about 1 minute. If the cake is not done, heat for an additional 15 seconds. Let the cake cool for a few minutes. If using, top with the whipped cream frosting and 1/2 teaspoon lemon zest. This cake is best consumed while still warm or within a few hours of being cooked.

Oven and Air Fryer Instructions

1. Preheat the oven or air fryer to 350°F (175°C).

2. In an oversized oven-safe mug (or a greased 8-ounce/240-ml oven-safe ramekin or similar sized oven-safe baking dish), combine the flour, baking powder, sugar, milk, oil, and vanilla. Mix with a small whisk until the batter is smooth. Add the 1 teaspoon lemon zest and the lemon curd and mix until the batter is smooth.

3. If using the oven, bake for 20 to 30 minutes, until a toothpick inserted comes out clean. If using the air fryer, bake for 10 to 15 minutes, until a toothpick inserted comes out clean. Let the cake cool for a few minutes. If using, top with the whipped cream frosting and 1/2 teaspoon lemon zest. This cake is best consumed while still warm or within a few hours of being cooked.

Apple Butter

This moist and fruity cake will definitely get you in the mood for fall, thanks to the use of fresh apples and flavorful apple butter.

SERVES 1 OR 2

¼ cup (30 g) all-purpose flour

¼ teaspoon baking powder

2 teaspoons granulated sugar

2½ tablespoons fat-free milk

½ tablespoon canola or avocado oil

2 tablespoons apple butter, divided

1 tablespoon diced apple

Microwave Instructions

1. In an oversized microwave-safe mug, combine the flour, baking powder, sugar, milk, oil, and 1 tablespoon of the apple butter. Mix with a small whisk until the batter is smooth. Stir in the diced apple. Swirl in the remaining 1 tablespoon apple butter with a fork.
2. Microwave for about 1 minute. If the cake is not done, heat for an additional 15 seconds. Let the cake cool for a few minutes. This cake is best consumed while still warm or within a few hours of being cooked.

Oven and Air Fryer Instructions

1. Preheat the oven or air fryer to 350°F (175°C).
2. In an oversized oven-safe mug (or a greased 8-ounce/240-ml oven-safe ramekin or similar sized oven-safe baking dish), combine the flour, baking powder, sugar, milk, oil, and 1 tablespoon of the apple butter. Mix with a small whisk until the batter is smooth. Stir in the diced apple. Swirl in the remaining 1 tablespoon apple butter with a fork.
3. If using the oven, bake for 20 to 30 minutes, until a toothpick inserted comes out clean. If using the air fryer, bake for 10 to 15 minutes, until a toothpick inserted comes out clean. Let the cake cool for a few minutes. This cake is best consumed while still warm or within a few hours of being cooked.

Tropical Island

Get a taste of tropical paradise with this cake, which is flavored with mango, coconut, and pineapple.

SERVES 1 OR 2

¼ cup (30 g) all-purpose flour

¼ teaspoon baking powder

2 teaspoons granulated sugar

3 tablespoons coconut milk

½ tablespoon canola or avocado oil

¼ teaspoon vanilla extract

1 tablespoon sweetened coconut flakes

1 tablespoon chopped ripe mangoes (see Note)

1 tablespoon diced canned pineapple (see Note)

Microwave Instructions

1. In an oversized microwave-safe mug, combine the flour, baking powder, sugar, milk, oil, and vanilla. Mix with a small whisk until the batter is smooth. Stir in the coconut flakes, mango, and pineapple.
2. Microwave for about 1 minute. If the cake is not done, heat for an additional 15 seconds. Let the cake cool for a few minutes. This cake is best consumed while still warm or within a few hours of being cooked.

Oven and Air Fryer Instructions

1. Preheat the oven or air fryer to 350°F (175°C).
2. In an oversized oven-safe mug (or a greased 8-ounce/240-ml oven-safe ramekin or similar sized oven-safe baking dish), combine the flour, baking powder, sugar, milk, oil, and vanilla. Mix with a small whisk until the batter is smooth. Stir in the coconut flakes, mango, and pineapple.
3. If using the oven, bake for 20 to 30 minutes, until a toothpick inserted comes out clean. If using the air fryer, bake for 10 to 15 minutes, until a toothpick inserted comes out clean. Let the cake cool for a few minutes. This cake is best consumed while still warm or within a few hours of being cooked.

*Note

You can add or replace the fruits listed with other chopped tropical fruits like lychee, guava, and papaya.

Healthy Snack Cakes

This section is devoted to cakes that are made without wheat flour, refined sugar, butter, or oil. Whether you are trying to eat a little healthier or baking for someone with a food allergy, you'll find plenty of delicious recipes, so no one needs to miss out.

Creamy Yogurt

Think cheesecake but made with yogurt instead. This is creamy, tangy, and lightly sweet. And, if baked in the air fryer, it develops an especially beautiful, caramelized surface. Feel free to adjust the amount of maple syrup to your liking.

Oven and Air Fryer Instructions

1. Preheat the oven to 350°F (175°C) or the air fryer to 320°F (160°C). Grease a 6-inch (15 cm) round baking pan with nonstick cooking spray and line it with parchment paper.

2. In a large bowl, whisk together the yogurt, eggs, and maple syrup until fully combined and no egg streaks remain. Sift in the cornstarch, 1 tablespoon at a time, whisking to fully incorporate after each addition. Transfer the batter to the prepared baking pan.

3. If using the oven, bake for 1 hour to 1 hour and 15 minutes, until puffed up and set, and the surface is caramelized. If using the air fryer, bake for 23 to 26 minutes, until puffed up and set (it should not be jiggly or liquidy) and the surface is caramelized. Let cool at room temperature for about 30 minutes. (The cake will deflate a bit as it's cooling.)

4. Refrigerate the cake for at least 2 hours or up to overnight so the flavors can fully develop (the texture will also firm up slightly).

5. Let the cake sit at room temperature for 15 to 30 minutes before serving. If using, drizzle with honey and decorate with fresh berries. Store any leftovers in the fridge in an airtight container.

SERVES 6 TO 8

1⅔ cups (400 g) plain nonfat Greek yogurt

4 large eggs

4 to 6 tablespoons maple syrup

¼ cup (32 g) cornstarch (see Note)

Honey, for drizzling (optional)

Fresh berries, for decorating (optional)

✱ Note

Cornstarch is added to absorb the excess moisture from the yogurt. If you leave it out, your yogurt cake will "weep" and you will have liquid puddled around the bottom of the cake.

Banana Oat

This is a cross between soft baked oatmeal and cake. It gets its sweetness from the overripe bananas.

SERVES 6 TO 8

1/4 cup (60 ml) whole milk

2 large overripe bananas, plus ripe banana slices for decorating (optional)

1 1/2 cups (130 g) rolled oats

1 teaspoon baking powder

Oven and Air Fryer Instructions

1. Preheat the oven or air fryer to 350°F (175°C). Grease a 6-inch (15 cm) round baking pan with nonstick cooking spray.
2. To a food processor fitted with the knife blade, add the milk, overripe bananas, rolled oats, and baking powder. Process until the bananas are mostly mashed and the oats still have some texture. Transfer to the prepared baking pan and spread it into an even layer.
3. If using the oven, bake for 30 to 35 minutes, until a toothpick inserted comes out clean. If using the air fryer, bake for 10 to 15 minutes, until a toothpick inserted comes out clean. Let cool completely. Store any leftovers in the fridge or freezer in an airtight container.

Healthier Chocolate

This quick and easy chocolate cake is made without flour, refined sugar, butter, or oil. The texture is similar to a flourless chocolate cake but it is much less work.

SERVES 1 OR 2

1 large egg

1½ tablespoons unsweetened Dutch-process cocoa powder

2 tablespoons maple syrup

Microwave Instructions

1. In an oversized microwave-safe mug, combine the egg, cocoa powder, and maple syrup. Mix vigorously with a small whisk until the batter is smooth.
2. Microwave for about 1 minute. If the cake is not done, heat for an additional 15 seconds. Let the cake cool for a few hours to allow the flavors to develop. Store any leftovers in the fridge or freezer in an airtight container.

Oven and Air Fryer Instructions

1. Preheat the oven or air fryer to 350°F (175°C).
2. In an oversized oven-safe mug (or a greased 8-ounce/240-ml oven-safe ramekin or similar sized oven-safe baking dish), combine the egg, cocoa powder, and maple syrup. Mix vigorously with a small whisk until the batter is smooth.
3. If using the oven, bake for 20 to 30 minutes, until a toothpick inserted comes out clean. If using the air fryer, bake for 10 to 15 minutes, until a toothpick inserted comes out clean. Let the cake cool for a few hours to allow the flavors to develop. Store any leftovers in the fridge or freezer in an airtight container.

Blueberry Oat Muffin

This healthy blueberry oat muffin cake can be enjoyed for breakfast or a snack. It's soft and moist and packed with fresh blueberries.

SERVES 1 OR 2

¼ cup (23 g) oat flour

½ teaspoon baking powder

3 tablespoons whole milk

1 tablespoon maple syrup

10 fresh blueberries, divided

Microwave Instructions

1. In an oversized microwave-safe mug, combine the oat flour, baking powder, milk, and maple syrup. Mix with a small whisk until the batter is smooth. Stir in 5 of the blueberries and scatter the remaining 5 blueberries on top.
2. Microwave for about 1 minute and 20 seconds, until the cake pulls away from the sides of the mug. Let the cake cool for a few minutes. This cake is best consumed while still warm or within a few hours of being cooked.

Oven and Air Fryer Instructions

1. Preheat the oven to 350°F (175°C).
2. In an oversized oven-safe mug (or a greased 8-ounce/240-ml oven-safe ramekin or similar sized oven-safe baking dish), combine the oat flour, baking powder, milk, and maple syrup. Mix with a small whisk until the batter is smooth. Stir in 5 of the blueberries, then top with the remaining 5 blueberries.
3. If using the oven, bake for 20 to 30 minutes, until a toothpick inserted comes out clean. If using the air fryer, bake for 10 to 15 minutes, until a toothpick inserted comes out clean. Let the cake cool for a few minutes. This cake is best consumed while still warm or within a few hours of being cooked.

Chickpea Brownies

This protein-packed brownie has a unique, nutty flavor, thanks to the chickpeas. Make sure to use peanut butter that doesn't contain any added oils.

SERVES 8 TO 10

1 can (15 ounces/400 g) chickpeas, drained

½ cup (128 g) natural peanut butter

½ cup (120 ml) maple syrup

2 tablespoons oat flour

3 tablespoons unsweetened Dutch-process cocoa powder

¼ cup (33 g) dark chocolate chips, plus more for topping (optional)

Oven Instructions

1. Preheat the oven to 350°F (175°C). Grease a 4 by 8-inch (10 by 20 cm) or 5 by 9-inch (12 by 23 cm) loaf pan with nonstick cooking spray and line it with parchment paper.

2. In a food processor fitted with the blade attachment, pulse the chickpeas until finely ground. Add the peanut butter, maple syrup, and oat flour and process at high speed until evenly combined and completely smooth, scraping down the sides with a spatula as needed. The batter will be quite thick. Add the cocoa powder and process until completely incorporated and the batter is uniform in color. Stir in the chocolate chips with a spatula. Transfer the batter to the prepared baking dish and spread it in an even layer. If using, top with additional chocolate chips.

3. Bake for 30 to 35 minutes, until the edges are browned and the surface looks slightly cracked. Let cool completely. Store any leftovers in the fridge or freezer in an airtight container.

Oatmeal

This oatmeal cake can be enjoyed for breakfast, snacktime, or dessert. You can also customize the cake with different mix-ins for more flavor, texture, or sweetness.

SERVES 6 TO 8

1½ cups (352 g) pureed bananas (about 2½ large bananas)

½ tablespoon baking powder

3 tablespoons maple syrup

1½ cups (135 g) rolled oats

Oven and Air Fryer Instructions

1. Preheat the oven or air fryer to 350°F (175°C). Grease a 6-inch (15 cm) round baking pan with nonstick cooking spray and line it with parchment paper.
2. In a large bowl, whisk together the pureed bananas and the baking powder until fully combined. Whisk in the maple syrup until fully combined. Add the oats and stir with a spatula until evenly incorporated. Transfer the batter to the prepared baking pan.
3. If using the oven, bake for about 30 minutes, or until the surface looks dry and the cake feels firm when gently pressed. If using the air fryer, bake for 10 to 15 minutes, until the surface looks dry and the cake feels firm when gently pressed. Let cool completely before slicing. Store any leftovers in the fridge or freezer in an airtight container.

Banana Oatmeal Bars

These banana oatmeal bars are soft, chewy, and lightly sweet. They are great for an on-the-go breakfast or snack. I also like to keep a batch in the freezer so I can have one whenever the craving strikes!

SERVES 8 TO 10

½ cup (115 g) finely mashed overripe bananas (about 1 large banana)

1 large egg

2 tablespoons maple syrup

1 cup (87 g) rolled oats

Oven and Air Fryer Instructions

1. Preheat the oven or air fryer to 350°F (175°C). Line a 4 by 8-inch (10 by 20 cm) loaf pan with parchment paper.
2. In a large bowl, whisk together the mashed bananas and the egg until fully incorporated and no egg streaks remain. Whisk in the maple syrup. Add the oats and stir with a spatula until evenly incorporated. Transfer to the prepared loaf pan and spread into an even layer.
3. If using the oven, bake for 20 to 30 minutes, until lightly golden and set. If using the air fryer, bake for 10 to 15 minutes, until lightly golden and set. Let cool completely. Store any leftovers in the fridge or freezer in an airtight container.

*Note

Want to add more flavor, texture, or sweetness? These bars taste great with chocolate chips or dried fruit mixed in. Just stir them in after you've mixed in the oats!

4-Ingredients-or-Fewer Snack Cakes

Do you shy away from recipes with long lists of ingredients? Problem solved! These recipes are the ultimate no-fuss desserts: They're ready in five minutes and they use only four ingredients or less. Say goodbye to lengthy shopping lists and get into the kitchen to make your cake and eat it too!

3-Ingredient Chocolate Bread

All you need for this moist, chocolatey quickbread cake is flour, baking powder, and some super-premium chocolate ice cream.

SERVES 1 OR 2

¼ cup (50 g) super-premium chocolate ice cream (not low-fat or fat-free; see Notes)

2 tablespoons all-purpose flour

¼ teaspoon baking powder

Whipped Cream Frosting (page 183), for topping (optional)

10 raspberries, for decorating (optional)

Notes

Make sure to use a super-premium, full-fat ice cream (like Häagen-Dazs); otherwise, it won't work.

Create your own variations with different ice cream flavors. Just make sure to choose strong flavors like espresso, chocolate, or caramel.

Microwave Instructions

1. In an oversized microwave-safe mug, microwave the ice cream for about 20 seconds, or until completely melted. Add the flour and baking powder. Mix with a small whisk until the batter is smooth.
2. Microwave for about 1 minute. If necessary, heat for an additional 15 seconds. Let cool for a few minutes.
3. If using, top with the whipped cream frosting and decorate with the raspberries. Store any leftovers in the fridge or freezer in an airtight container.

Oven and Air Fryer Instructions

1. Preheat the oven or air fryer to 350°F (175°C).
2. In an oversized microwave-safe mug, microwave the ice cream for about 20 seconds, or until completely melted. Add the flour and baking powder. Mix with a small whisk until the batter is smooth.
3. If the mug is oven-safe, bake the cake in it. If not, transfer the batter to a greased 8-ounce (240 ml) oven-safe ramekin or similar sized oven-safe baking dish. If using the oven, bake for 20 to 30 minutes, until a toothpick inserted comes out clean. If using the air fryer, bake for 10 to 15 minutes, until a toothpick inserted comes out clean. Let cool for a few minutes.
4. If using, top with the whipped cream frosting and decorate with the raspberries. Store any leftovers in the fridge or freezer in an airtight container.

2-Ingredient Oreo Chocolate

This cake is rich, soft, moist, and so easy to make. Just blend Oreos and water!

SERVES 6 TO 8

28 Oreo cookies

1 cup (240 ml) room temperature water

Microwave Instructions

1. Grease a 6-inch (15 cm) round silicone cake mold or similar-sized microwave-safe baking dish with nonstick cooking spray.
2. To a blender, add the Oreo cookies and 1 cup (240 ml) of water. Blend at high speed until the batter is smooth. Transfer the batter to the prepared mold or baking dish.
3. Microwave for 6 minutes, until a toothpick inserted comes out clean. Let cool completely. Store any leftovers in the fridge or freezer in an airtight container.

3-Ingredient Flourless Nutella

This is a version of my viral Nutella cake recipe that was posted on my blog, *Kirbie's Cravings*. I've adapted that recipe here for an even easier Nutella mug cake, and the results are just as rich and delicious as the original.

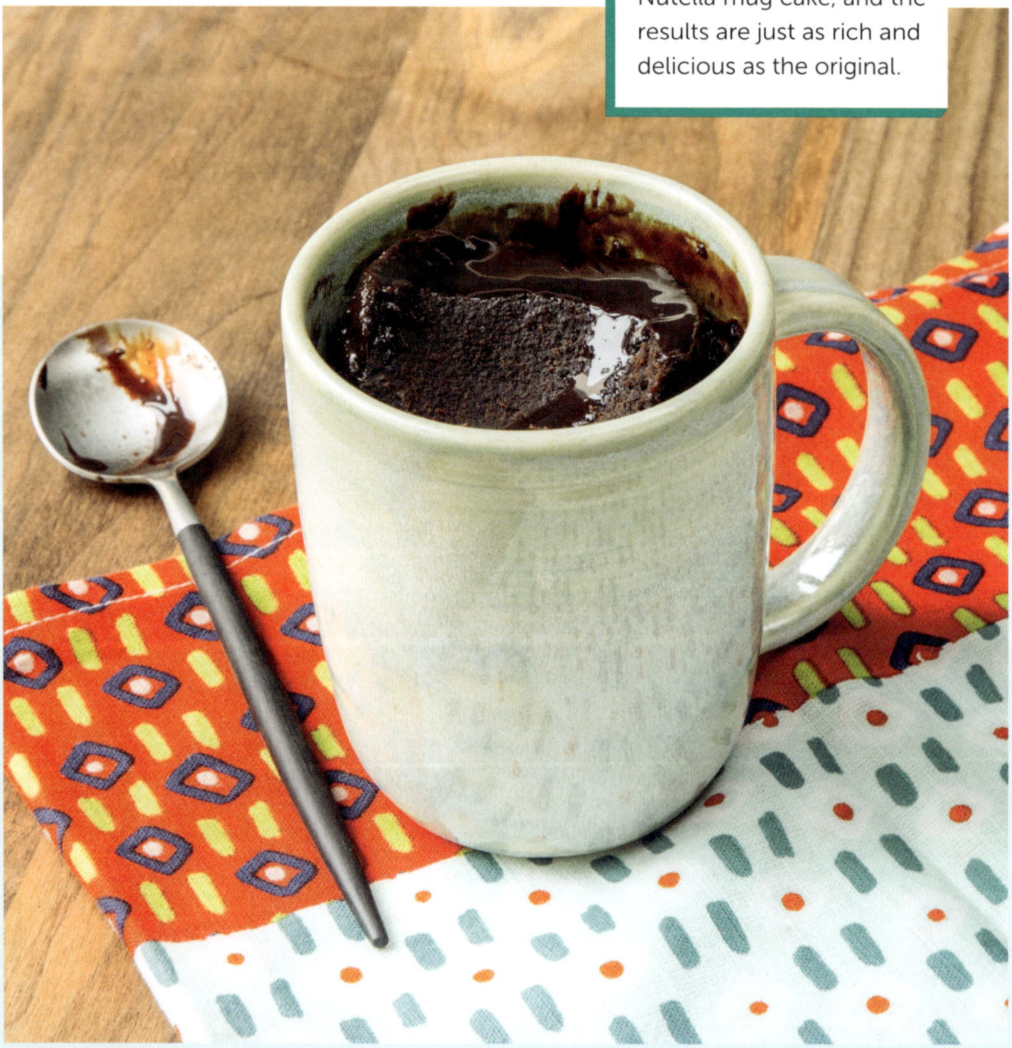

SERVES 1 OR 2

1 large egg

1/4 cup (74 g) Nutella

1/2 tablespoon unsweetened Dutch-process cocoa powder

Chocolate Ganache Frosting (page 182), for topping (optional)

Chopped walnuts, for topping (optional)

Microwave Instructions

1. In an oversized microwave-safe mug, combine the egg, Nutella, and cocoa powder. Mix vigorously with a small whisk until the batter is smooth and the egg is fully incorporated. (Because the mixture is so dark, it will be hard to see if egg streaks remain. Lift your whisk a couple times to make sure you don't see evidence of unmixed egg still in the batter.)
2. Microwave for about 1 minute and 10 seconds. The cake will look the slightest bit gooey on top, but as long as the cake has risen and is set, it should be ready. Let cool completely, so the chocolate hazelnut flavor can fully develop. If using, top with the chocolate ganache frosting and chopped walnuts. Store any leftovers in the fridge or freezer in an airtight container.

Oven and Air Fryer Instructions

1. Preheat the oven or air fryer to 350°F (175°C).
2. In an oversized oven-safe mug (or a greased 8-ounce/240-ml oven-safe ramekin or similar sized oven-safe baking dish), combine the egg, Nutella, and cocoa powder. Mix vigorously with a small whisk until the batter is smooth and the egg is fully incorporated. (Because the mixture is so dark, it will be hard to see if egg streaks remain. Lift your whisk a couple times to make sure you don't see evidence of unmixed egg still in the batter.)
3. If using the oven, bake for 20 to 30 minutes, until a toothpick inserted comes out clean. If using the air fryer, bake for 10 to 15 minutes, until a toothpick inserted comes out clean. Let cool completely, so the chocolate hazelnut flavor can fully develop. If using, top with the chocolate ganache frosting and chopped walnuts. Store any leftovers in the fridge or freezer in an airtight container.

4-Ingredient Nutella

This cake is for my fellow Nutella superfans. It's incredibly moist, rich, and really allows the creamy chocolate hazelnut spread to be the star. You won't believe it's only four ingredients.

SERVES 1 OR 2

¼ cup (30 g) all-purpose flour

¼ teaspoon baking powder

3 tablespoons fat-free milk

¼ cup (74 g) Nutella

Microwave Instructions

1. In an oversized microwave-safe mug, combine the flour, baking powder, milk, and Nutella. Mix vigorously with a small whisk until the batter is smooth.
2. Microwave for about 1 minute. If the cake is not done, heat for an additional 15 seconds. Let the cake cool for a few minutes. This cake is best consumed while still warm or within a few hours of being cooked.

Oven and Air Fryer Instructions

1. Preheat the oven or air fryer to 350°F (175°C).
2. In an oversized oven-safe mug (or a greased 8-ounce/240-ml oven-safe ramekin or similar sized oven-safe baking dish), combine the flour, baking powder, milk, and Nutella. Mix vigorously with a small whisk until the batter is smooth.
3. If using the oven, bake for 20 to 30 minutes, until a toothpick inserted comes out clean. If using the air fryer, bake for 10 to 15 minutes, until a toothpick inserted comes out clean. Let the cake cool for a few minutes. This cake is best consumed while still warm or within a few hours of being cooked.

4-Ingredient Peanut Butter

This cake is so creamy and full of peanut butter flavor, and has a texture like a cake made with flour—but it doesn't contain any!

SERVES 6 TO 8

½ cup (128 g) regular creamy peanut butter

4 large eggs

¼ cup plus 2 tablespoons (75 g) granulated sugar

1 teaspoon baking powder

Oven and Air Fryer Instructions

1. Preheat the oven or air fryer to 350°F (175°C). Grease a 6-inch (15 cm) round baking pan with nonstick cooking spray and line it with parchment paper.
2. In a large bowl, whisk together the peanut butter, eggs, sugar, and baking powder until fully incorporated and no egg streaks remain. Transfer to the prepared baking pan.
3. If using the oven, bake for 25 to 30 minutes, until a toothpick inserted comes out clean. If using the air fryer, bake for 10 to 15 minutes, until a toothpick inserted comes out clean. Let cool completely. Store any leftovers in the fridge or freezer in an airtight container.

Breakfast Snack Cakes

Is breakfast your favorite meal of the day? If so, you're in for a treat. This chapter features fun twists on breakfast favorites, from Blueberry Muffin Streusel (page 73) to a Giant Pancake (page 74) to French Toast (page 75). But don't let the time of day dictate your breakfast cravings—breakfast can happen anywhere, at any time. Especially when it's this delicious.

Coffee Streusel

This sour cream–based cake has tangy undertones and is covered with a buttery cinnamon streusel topping.

SERVES 1 OR 2

1/4 cup (30 g) all-purpose flour

1/4 teaspoon baking powder

3 teaspoons granulated sugar

2 tablespoons fat-free milk

1/2 tablespoon canola or avocado oil

2 tablespoons sour cream

Streusel Topping (page 185)

Microwave Instructions

1. In an oversized microwave-safe mug, combine the flour, baking powder, sugar, milk, oil, and sour cream. Mix with a small whisk until the batter is smooth. Sprinkle the streusel evenly across the top.
2. Microwave for about 1 minute. If the cake is not done, heat for an additional 15 seconds. This cake is best consumed while still warm or within a few hours of being cooked.

Oven and Air Fryer Instructions

1. Preheat the oven or air fryer to 350°F (175°C).
2. In an oversized oven-safe mug (or a greased 8-ounce/240-ml oven-safe ramekin or similar sized oven-safe baking dish), combine the flour, baking powder, sugar, milk, oil, and sour cream. Mix with a small whisk until the batter is smooth. Sprinkle the streusel evenly across the top.
3. If using the oven, bake for 20 to 30 minutes, until a toothpick inserted comes out clean. If using the air fryer, bake for 10 to 15 minutes, until a toothpick inserted comes out clean. This cake is best consumed while still warm or within a few hours of being cooked.

Espresso

Why not add your morning cup of coffee directly into your breakfast? Many baked goods contain espresso powder to deepen the flavor, but this one lets the coffee be the star.

SERVES 1 OR 2

¼ cup (30 g) all-purpose flour

¼ teaspoon baking powder

3 teaspoons granulated sugar

3 tablespoons fat-free milk

½ tablespoon canola or avocado oil

½ teaspoon espresso powder

½ teaspoon confectioners' sugar, for topping (optional)

Microwave Instructions

1. In an oversized microwave-safe mug, combine the flour, baking powder, granulated sugar, milk, oil, and espresso powder. Mix with a small whisk until the batter is smooth.
2. Microwave for about 1 minute. If the cake is not done, heat for an additional 15 seconds. Let cool for a few minutes.
3. If using, dust with confectioners' sugar. This cake is best consumed while still warm or within a few hours of being cooked.

Oven and Air Fryer Instructions

1. Preheat the oven or air fryer to 350°F (175°C).
2. In an oversized oven-safe mug (or a greased 8-ounce/240-ml oven-safe ramekin or similar sized oven-safe baking dish), combine the flour, baking powder, sugar, milk, oil, and espresso powder. Mix with a small whisk until the batter is smooth.
3. If using the oven, bake for 20 to 30 minutes, until a toothpick inserted comes out clean. If using the air fryer, bake for 10 to 15 minutes, until a toothpick inserted comes out clean. Let cool for a few minutes.
4. If using, dust with confectioners' sugar. This cake is best consumed while still warm or within a few hours of being cooked.

Blueberry Muffin Streusel

This muffin cake is studded with blueberries and covered with a generous amount of streusel. It takes a little more effort if you want to add the topping, but streusel is always worth it, at least in my book!

SERVES 1 OR 2

¼ cup (30 g) all-purpose flour

⅛ teaspoon baking powder

Pinch baking soda

2 teaspoons granulated sugar

3 tablespoons fat-free milk

½ tablespoon canola or avocado oil

8 blueberries

Streusel Topping (page 185; see Note)

Microwave Instructions

1. In an oversized microwave-safe mug, combine the flour, baking powder, baking soda, sugar, milk, and oil. Mix with a small whisk until the batter is smooth. Stir in the blueberries. Sprinkle the streusel evenly across the top.
2. Microwave for about 1 minute. If the cake is not done, heat for an additional 15 seconds. This cake is best consumed while still warm or within a few hours of being cooked.

Oven and Air Fryer Instructions

1. Preheat the oven or air fryer to 350°F (175°C).
2. In an oversized oven-safe mug (or a greased 8-ounce/240-ml oven-safe ramekin or similar sized oven-safe baking dish), combine the flour, baking powder, baking soda, sugar, milk, and oil. Mix with a small whisk until the batter is smooth. Stir in the blueberries. Sprinkle the streusel evenly across the top.
3. If using the oven, bake for 20 to 30 minutes, until a toothpick inserted comes out clean. If using the air fryer, bake for 10 to 15 minutes, until a toothpick inserted comes out clean. This cake is best consumed while still warm or within a few hours of being cooked.

*Note

If you don't care for streusel, you can just exclude it and save some time. Or you can sprinkle coarse sugar on top as an alternative.

Giant Pancake

My ideal breakfast almost always involves pancakes. With this recipe, there's no need to hover over the stove flipping.

SERVES 8 TO 10

1 cup (125 g) all-purpose flour

3 tablespoons granulated sugar

¾ teaspoon baking powder

¾ teaspoon baking soda

1¼ cups (300 ml) buttermilk

1 large egg

1½ tablespoons canola or avocado oil

Whipped cream, for topping (optional)

Honey or maple syrup, for drizzling (optional)

Fresh fruit, for topping (optional)

Oven Instructions

1. Preheat the oven to 350°F (175°C). Grease a 7-inch (18 cm) springform cake pan with butter.

2. In a large bowl, whisk together the flour, sugar, baking powder, and baking soda until well combined. Add the buttermilk, egg, and oil. Whisk until only small lumps remain. Be careful not to overmix the batter. Transfer to the prepared cake pan.

3. Bake for 40 to 45 minutes, until golden brown and a toothpick inserted comes out clean. Let cool for a few minutes before removing from the pan. Serve with whipped cream, honey or maple syrup, and fresh fruit, as desired.

French Toast

Breakfast just got a whole lot simpler with this easy microwave French toast mug cake. It's also a good use of day-old bread.

SERVES 1 OR 2

1 slice of bread (either white or wheat), cut into ½-inch (6 mm) cubes

2 tablespoons beaten egg (½ large egg; see Note)

2 tablespoons fat-free milk

⅛ teaspoon ground cinnamon

1 tablespoon granulated sugar

Maple syrup, for serving

Microwave Instructions

1. Line the walls of an oversized microwave-safe mug with bread cubes, then fill the middle to form a bread cube tower.
2. In a separate mug or small bowl, mix the egg, milk, cinnamon, and sugar with a small whisk. Pour the mixture onto the bread cubes, making sure the batter touches all of them.
3. Microwave for about 1 minute, or until the egg-custard mixture is completely cooked. Let the cake cool for a few minutes. You can eat straight from the mug or easily transfer the tower of French toast onto a plate. Serve with maple syrup.

***Note**

If you don't want to waste part of an egg, you can easily make two servings of this cake with one large egg.

Donut

This cake is soft, moist, and tastes like old-fashioned cake donuts (thanks to the addition of a little nutmeg). It always takes me back to my childhood.

SERVES 1 OR 2

- 1/4 cup plus 2 tablespoons (75 g) all-purpose flour
- 3 tablespoons granulated sugar
- 1/2 teaspoon baking powder
- Pinch ground nutmeg
- 2 tablespoons canola or avocado oil
- 3 tablespoons fat-free milk
- 1/4 teaspoon vanilla extract
- Chocolate Ganache Frosting (page 182), for topping (optional)
- Vanilla Glaze (page 185), for topping (optional)
- Sprinkles, for decorating (optional)

Microwave Instructions

1. In an oversized microwave-safe mug, combine the flour, sugar, baking powder, nutmeg, oil, milk, and vanilla. Mix with a small whisk until the batter is smooth.
2. Microwave for about 1 minute. If the cake is not done, heat for an additional 15 seconds.
3. If using, top with the chocolate ganache or vanilla glaze and decorate with sprinkles. This cake is best consumed while still warm or within a few hours of being cooked.

Oven and Air Fryer Instructions

1. Preheat the oven or air fryer to 350°F (175°C).
2. In an oversized oven-safe mug (or a greased 8-ounce/240-ml oven-safe ramekin or similar sized oven-safe baking dish), combine the flour, sugar, baking powder, nutmeg, oil, milk, and vanilla. Mix with a small whisk until the batter is smooth.
3. If using the oven, bake for 20 to 30 minutes, until a toothpick inserted comes out clean. If using the air fryer, bake for 10 to 15 minutes, until a toothpick inserted comes out clean. Let the cake cool a few minutes.
4. If using, top with the chocolate ganache or vanilla glaze and decorate with sprinkles. This cake is best consumed while still warm or within a few hours of being cooked.

Banana Bread

When you don't want to wait for banana bread to bake, there's my instant microwave banana bread, which only takes five minutes. And if you have more time, you can use the oven or air fryer.

SERVES 1 OR 2

¼ cup (30 g) all-purpose flour

½ teaspoon baking powder

2 teaspoons granulated sugar

2½ tablespoons fat-free milk

½ tablespoon canola or avocado oil

⅛ teaspoon ground cinnamon

2 tablespoons mashed overripe banana (about ½ large banana; see Note), plus fresh banana slices, for topping (optional)

1 tablespoon chopped pecans or walnuts (optional)

* Note

The more overripe the banana, the easier it will be to whisk. Also, avoid using frozen bananas as they retain a great amount of water that will make the cake gummy.

Microwave Instructions

1. In an oversized microwave-safe mug, combine the flour, baking powder, sugar, milk, oil, cinnamon, and mashed banana. Mix vigorously with a small whisk until smooth. If using, stir in the chopped nuts. Microwave for about 1 minute. If necessary, heat for an additional 15 seconds. Let cool for a few minutes.

2. If using, top with fresh banana slices. This cake is best consumed while still warm or within a few hours of being cooked.

Oven and Air Fryer Instructions

1. Preheat the oven or air fryer to 350°F (175°C).

2. In an oversized oven-safe mug (or a greased 8-ounce/240-ml oven-safe ramekin or similar sized oven-safe baking dish), combine the flour, baking powder, sugar, milk, oil, cinnamon, and mashed banana. Mix vigorously with a small whisk until smooth. If using, stir in the chopped nuts. If using the oven, bake for 20 to 30 minutes, until a toothpick inserted comes out clean. If using the air fryer, bake for 10 to 15 minutes, until a toothpick inserted comes out clean. Let cool for a few minutes.

3. If using, top with fresh banana slices. This cake is best consumed while still warm or within a few hours of being cooked.

Honey Swirl

Honey cake is so simple and charming in its simplicity. I enjoy eating this cake over a leisurely weekend breakfast with a cup of steaming hot tea.

SERVES 1 OR 2

¼ cup (30 g) all-purpose flour

¼ teaspoon baking powder

3 teaspoons granulated sugar

3 tablespoons fat-free milk

½ tablespoon canola or avocado oil

1½ tablespoons honey, divided

Microwave Instructions

1. In an oversized microwave-safe mug, combine the flour, baking powder, sugar, milk, oil, and 1 tablespoon of the honey. Mix with a small whisk until smooth. Swirl in the remaining ½ tablespoon honey with a fork. (Don't mix it in completely because you want to maintain the swirls of honey.)

2. Microwave for about 1 minute. If necessary, heat for an additional 15 seconds. This cake is best consumed while still warm or within a few hours of being cooked.

Oven and Air Fryer Instructions

1. Preheat the oven or air fryer to 350°F (175°C).

2. In an oversized oven-safe mug (or a greased 8-ounce/240-ml oven-safe ramekin or similar sized oven-safe baking dish), combine the flour, baking powder, sugar, milk, oil, and 1 tablespoon of the honey. Mix with a small whisk until smooth. Swirl in the remaining ½ tablespoon honey with a fork. (Don't mix it in completely because you want to maintain the swirls of honey.)

3. If using the oven, bake for 20 to 30 minutes, until a toothpick inserted comes out clean. If using the air fryer, bake for 10 to 15 minutes, until a toothpick inserted comes out clean. This cake is best consumed while still warm or within a few hours of being cooked.

Coffee & Tea Snack Cakes

Whether you're a coffee addict or tea connoisseur, this chapter has you covered—now you can get your favorite caffeine fix in edible form! I consume both beverages daily, and the only thing I love more than drinking them is eating sweets flavored with them. These coffee and tea mug cakes are good to the last drop—*errrr*, bite!

Gingerbread-Spice Latte

Add a little spice to your day with this scrumptious winter-season snack. The popular holiday drink is turned into a cake, with hints of molasses, ginger, and espresso.

SERVES 1 OR 2

¼ cup (30 g) all-purpose flour

¼ teaspoon baking powder

1 tablespoon packed dark brown sugar

¼ teaspoon espresso powder

½ teaspoon ground ginger

Pinch ground cinnamon

3 tablespoons fat-free milk

½ tablespoon canola or avocado oil

1 tablespoon dark molasses

Microwave Instructions

1. In an oversized microwave-safe mug, combine the flour, baking powder, brown sugar, espresso powder, ginger, cinnamon, milk, oil, and molasses. Mix with a small whisk until the batter is smooth.
2. Microwave for about 1 minute. If the cake is not done, heat for an additional 15 seconds. Let the cake cool for a few minutes. This cake is best consumed while still warm or within a few hours of being cooked.

Oven and Air Fryer Instructions

1. Preheat the oven or air fryer to 350°F (175°C).
2. In an oversized oven-safe mug (or a greased 8-ounce/240-ml oven-safe ramekin or similar sized oven-safe baking dish), combine the flour, baking powder, brown sugar, espresso powder, ginger, cinnamon, milk, oil, and molasses. Mix with a small whisk until the batter is smooth.
3. If using the oven, bake for 20 to 30 minutes, until a toothpick inserted comes out clean. If using the air fryer, bake for 10 to 15 minutes, until a toothpick inserted comes out clean. Let the cake cool for a few minutes. This cake is best consumed while still warm or within a few hours of being cooked.

Java Chip

Inspired by the popular Starbucks' drink, this is an espresso-flavored cake studded with bittersweet chocolate chips. I like to top mine off with whipped cream.

SERVES 1 OR 2

1/4 cup (30 g) all-purpose flour

1/4 teaspoon baking powder

1 tablespoon granulated sugar

1/2 teaspoon espresso powder

3 tablespoons fat-free milk

1/2 tablespoon canola or avocado oil

1 heaping tablespoon mini bittersweet chocolate chips

Whipped cream, for topping (optional)

Microwave Instructions

1. In an oversized microwave-safe mug, combine the flour, baking powder, sugar, espresso powder, milk, and oil. Mix with a small whisk until the batter is smooth. Stir in the chocolate chips.
2. Microwave for about 1 minute. If the cake is not done, heat for an additional 15 seconds. Let the cake cool for a few minutes.
3. If using, top with whipped cream. This cake is best consumed while still warm or within a few hours of being cooked.

Oven and Air Fryer Instructions

1. Preheat the oven or air fryer to 350°F (175°C).
2. In an oversized oven-safe mug (or a greased 8-ounce/240-ml oven-safe ramekin or similar sized oven-safe baking dish), combine the flour, baking powder, sugar, espresso powder, milk, and oil. Mix with a small whisk until the batter is smooth. Stir in the chocolate chips.
3. If using the oven, bake for 20 to 30 minutes, until a toothpick inserted comes out clean. If using the air fryer, bake for 10 to 15 minutes, until a toothpick inserted comes out clean. Let the cake cool for a few minutes.
4. If using, top with whipped cream. This cake is best consumed while still warm or within a few hours of being cooked.

Matcha Green Tea

Matcha is a green tea powder that brings a natural, vibrant green hue to this cake. The unique and complex flavor of matcha truly comes through, and it has a lot of health benefits as well—which is a great justification for eating this yummy mug cake!

SERVES 1 OR 2

¼ cup (30 g) all-purpose flour

1 teaspoon ceremonial grade matcha powder (see Note)

¼ teaspoon baking powder

1 tablespoon granulated sugar

3 tablespoons fat-free milk

½ tablespoon canola or avocado oil

Microwave Instructions

1. In an oversized microwave-safe mug, combine the flour, matcha, baking powder, and sugar. Mix with a small whisk until evenly incorporated. Add the milk and oil and whisk until the batter is smooth and no matcha powder clumps remain (a few dark green specks are okay, but you don't want any lumps).
2. Microwave for about 1 minute. If the cake is not done, heat for an additional 15 seconds. Let the cake cool for a few minutes. This cake is best consumed while still warm or within a few hours of being cooked.

Oven and Air Fryer Instructions

1. Preheat the oven or air fryer to 350°F (175°C).
2. In an oversized oven-safe mug (or a greased 8-ounce/240-ml oven-safe ramekin or similar sized oven-safe baking dish), combine the flour, matcha, baking powder, and sugar. Mix with a small whisk until evenly incorporated. Add the milk and oil and whisk until the batter is smooth and no matcha powder clumps remain (a few dark green specks are okay, but you don't want any lumps).
3. If using the oven, bake for 20 to 30 minutes, until a toothpick inserted comes out clean. If using the air fryer, bake for 10 to 15 minutes, until a toothpick inserted comes out clean. Let the cake cool for a few minutes. This cake is best consumed while still warm or within a few hours of being cooked.

*Note

Use ceremonial grade matcha powder meant for tea ceremonies and not the culinary-grade version if you want a pretty green-colored cake. The lower quality matcha powders will make the cake more of a yellowish green.

Mocha

A little bit of chocolate makes everything taste better, which is probably why mocha is such a popular coffee beverage. This cake is made with espresso powder and just a touch of cocoa.

SERVES 1 OR 2

3 tablespoons all-purpose flour

¼ teaspoon baking powder

2 tablespoons granulated sugar

1 tablespoon unsweetened Dutch-process cocoa powder

1 teaspoon espresso powder

3 tablespoons fat-free milk

½ tablespoon canola or avocado oil

Microwave Instructions

1. In an oversized microwave-safe mug, combine the flour, baking powder, sugar, cocoa powder, espresso powder, milk, and oil. Mix with a small whisk until the batter is smooth.
2. Microwave for about 1 minute. If the cake is not done, heat for an additional 15 seconds. Let the cake cool for a few minutes. This cake is best consumed while still warm or within a few hours of being cooked.

Oven and Air Fryer Instructions

1. Preheat the oven or air fryer to 350°F (175°C).
2. In an oversized oven-safe mug (or a greased 8-ounce/240-ml oven-safe ramekin or similar sized oven-safe baking dish), combine the flour, baking powder, sugar, cocoa powder, espresso powder, milk, and oil. Mix with a small whisk until the batter is smooth.
3. If using the oven, bake for 20 to 30 minutes, until a toothpick inserted comes out clean. If using the air fryer, bake for 10 to 15 minutes, until a toothpick inserted comes out clean. Let the cake cool for a few minutes. This cake is best consumed while still warm or within a few hours of being cooked.

Pumpkin Spice Latte

A touch of pumpkin, a dash of spice, a shot of espresso, and a generous pour of creamy milk— the pumpkin-spice latte is the quintessential fall beverage. I've created a cake that's just as pleasurable as the drink.

SERVES 1 OR 2

¼ cup (30 g) all-purpose flour

¼ teaspoon baking powder

2 tablespoons granulated sugar

½ teaspoon pumpkin spice

¼ teaspoon espresso powder

2 tablespoons canned pumpkin puree

2 tablespoons fat-free milk

½ tablespoon canola or avocado oil

Microwave Instructions

1. In an oversized microwave-safe mug, combine the flour, baking powder, sugar, pumpkin spice, espresso powder, pumpkin, milk, and oil. Mix vigorously with a small whisk until the batter is smooth.
2. Microwave for about 1 minute 30 seconds. If the cake is not done, heat for an additional 15 seconds. Let the cake cool for a few minutes. This cake is best consumed while still warm or within a few hours of being cooked.

Oven and Air Fryer Instructions

1. Preheat the oven or air fryer to 350°F (175°C).
2. In an oversized oven-safe mug (or a greased 8-ounce/240-ml oven-safe ramekin or similar sized oven-safe baking dish), combine the flour, baking powder, sugar, pumpkin spice, espresso powder, pumpkin, milk, and oil. Mix vigorously with a small whisk until the batter is smooth.
3. If using the oven, bake for 20 to 30 minutes, until a toothpick inserted comes out clean. If using the air fryer, bake for 10 to 15 minutes, until a toothpick inserted comes out clean. Let the cake cool for a few minutes. This cake is best consumed while still warm or within a few hours of being cooked.

Thai Tea

Thai iced tea is one of my favorite beverages. This cake produces the same brilliant shade of orange as the drink. Make sure to use an instant Thai tea mix that has sugar and cream in the powder.

SERVES 1 OR 2

¼ cup (30 g) all-purpose flour

¼ teaspoon baking powder

1 tablespoon granulated sugar

1 tablespoon instant Thai tea mix (see Note)

3 tablespoons fat-free milk

½ tablespoon canola or avocado oil

Microwave Instructions

1. In an oversized microwave-safe mug, combine the flour, baking powder, sugar, Thai tea mix, milk, and oil. Mix with a small whisk until the batter is smooth.
2. Microwave for about 1 minute. If the cake is not done, heat for an additional 15 seconds. Let the cake cool for a few minutes. This cake is best consumed while still warm or within a few hours of being cooked.

Oven and Air Fryer Instructions

1. Preheat the oven or air fryer to 350°F (175°C).
2. In an oversized oven-safe mug (or a greased 8-ounce/240-ml oven-safe ramekin or similar sized oven-safe baking dish), combine the flour, baking powder, sugar, Thai tea mix, milk, and oil. Mix with a small whisk until the batter is smooth.
3. If using the oven, bake for 20 to 30 minutes, until a toothpick inserted comes out clean. If using the air fryer, bake for 10 to 15 minutes, until a toothpick inserted comes out clean. Let the cake cool for a few minutes. This cake is best consumed while still warm or within a few hours of being cooked.

*Note

Instant Thai tea mix packages can be purchased at most Asian grocery stores.

Vanilla Latte

Vanilla-flavored lattes may sound boring, but this cake is no wallflower. It's enhanced with vanilla bean paste, giving it a wonderfully aromatic finish.

SERVES 1 OR 2

¼ cup (30 g) all-purpose flour

¼ teaspoon baking powder

1 tablespoon granulated sugar

¼ teaspoon espresso powder

½ teaspoon vanilla bean paste

3 tablespoons fat-free milk

½ tablespoon canola or avocado oil

Microwave Instructions

1. In an oversized microwave-safe mug, combine the flour, baking powder, sugar, espresso powder, vanilla bean paste, milk, and oil. Mix with a small whisk until the batter is smooth.
2. Microwave for about 1 minute. If the cake is not done, heat for an additional 15 seconds. Let the cake cool for a few minutes. This cake is best consumed while still warm or within a few hours of being cooked.

Oven and Air Fryer Instructions

1. Preheat the oven or air fryer to 350°F (175°C).
2. In an oversized oven-safe mug (or a greased 8-ounce/240-ml oven-safe ramekin or similar sized oven-safe baking dish), combine the flour, baking powder, sugar, espresso powder, vanilla bean paste, milk, and oil. Mix with a small whisk until the batter is smooth.
3. If using the oven, bake for 20 to 30 minutes, until a toothpick inserted comes out clean. If using the air fryer, bake for 10 to 15 minutes, until a toothpick inserted comes out clean. Let the cake cool for a few minutes. This cake is best consumed while still warm or within a few hours of being cooked.

Nostalgic Snack Cakes

This section is a trip down memory lane, offering up confections you were likely first introduced to as a child—from s'mores to Jell-O to the much-loved Hostess Cupcakes. While we can't travel back in time, we can relive some precious moments through these cakes. And, of course, these recipes are also great to make and share with any kids in your life.

Hostess (Cup)cake

The flavors of a Hostess Cupcake are mimicked in this chocolate cake base and fluffy melted marshmallow–creme center.

Microwave Instructions

1. In an oversized microwave-safe mug, combine the flour, baking powder, sugar, cocoa powder, milk, and oil. Mix with a small whisk until the batter is smooth. Scoop out ¼ cup (60 ml) of the batter and set aside, leaving only a thin layer of batter at the bottom of the mug.
2. Add the marshmallow creme, making sure it's as close to the bottom as possible. Top the marshmallow creme with the remaining batter, making sure to completely cover the marshmallow. (The weight of the batter will help keep the creme in place during cooking.)
3. Microwave for about 1 minute. If the cake is not done, heat for an additional 15 seconds. Let the cake cool for a few minutes.
4. Top with the chocolate ganache frosting. Using a piping bag fitted with a round tip, pipe loops of cream cheese frosting across the top. Store any leftovers in the fridge or freezer in an airtight container.

SERVES 1 OR 2

3 tablespoons all-purpose flour

¼ teaspoon baking powder

1 tablespoon granulated sugar

1 tablespoon unsweetened Dutch-process cocoa powder

3 tablespoons fat-free milk

½ tablespoon canola or avocado oil

1 tablespoon marshmallow creme (such as Jet-Puffed or Fluff)

Chocolate Ganache Frosting (page 182), for topping

Cream Cheese Frosting (page 183), for decorating

Pudding

A few years ago, cake mix brands began adding pudding mix to their batter. The mix makes cakes extra moist, so I've adopted that trick. Just one scoop of the magic ingredient makes for an especially pleasurable experience.

SERVES 1 OR 2

3 tablespoons all-purpose flour

¼ teaspoon baking powder

2 teaspoons granulated sugar

1 tablespoon instant vanilla pudding mix (see Note)

3 tablespoons fat-free milk

½ tablespoon canola or avocado oil

Microwave Instructions

1. In an oversized microwave-safe mug, combine the flour, baking powder, sugar, pudding mix, milk, and oil. Mix with a small whisk until the batter is smooth.
2. Microwave for about 1 minute. If the cake is not done, heat for an additional 15 seconds. Let the cake cool for a few minutes. This cake is best consumed while still warm or within a few hours of being cooked.

Oven and Air Fryer Instructions

1. Preheat the oven or air fryer to 350°F (175°C).
2. In an oversized oven-safe mug (or a greased 8-ounce/240-ml oven-safe ramekin or similar sized oven-safe baking dish), combine the flour, baking powder, sugar, pudding mix, milk, and oil. Mix with a small whisk until the batter is smooth.
3. If using the oven, bake for 20 to 30 minutes, until a toothpick inserted comes out clean. If using the air fryer, bake for 10 to 15 minutes, until a toothpick inserted comes out clean. Let the cake cool for a few minutes. This cake is best consumed while still warm or within a few hours of being cooked.

*Note

I usually stick with vanilla pudding mix, but you can mix and match flavors as you like.

Snickerdoodle

Spiced with cinnamon, this soft and moist cake reminds me of a snickerdoodle cookie but in cake form.

SERVES 6 TO 8

3/4 cup (95 g) all-purpose flour

1 teaspoon baking powder

1/8 teaspoon salt

1/2 cup (58 g) light brown sugar, not packed

1 teaspoon ground cinnamon

2 1/2 tablespoons canola or avocado oil

Oven and Air Fryer Instructions

1. Preheat the oven or air fryer to 350°F (175°C). Grease a 6-inch round cake pan with butter or nonstick cooking spray.
2. In a large bowl, whisk together the flour, baking powder, salt, brown sugar, and cinnamon. Add the oil and 1/2 cup (120 ml) of water and whisk until the batter is smooth. Transfer to the prepared cake pan.
3. If using the oven, bake for 30 to 35 minutes, until a toothpick inserted comes out clean. If using the air fryer, bake the cake for about 12 to 18 minutes, until a toothpick inserted comes out clean. Let cool for 20 minutes, then transfer to a wire rack to cool completely. Store any leftovers in the fridge or freezer in an airtight container.

Funfetti

Funfetti was always my choice for a birthday cake when I was growing up. Colorful sprinkles melted into a simple white cake make this a festive party recipe for big kids and small kids alike. It's fun to look at and, of course, to eat.

SERVES 1 OR 2

¼ cup (30 g) all-purpose flour

¼ teaspoon baking powder

2 teaspoons granulated sugar

3 tablespoons fat-free milk

½ tablespoon canola or avocado oil

¼ teaspoon vanilla extract

½ tablespoon rainbow sprinkles, plus more for decorating (optional)

Vanilla ice cream, for topping (optional)

Microwave Instructions

1. In an oversized microwave-safe mug, combine the flour, baking powder, sugar, milk, oil, and vanilla. Mix with a small whisk until the batter is smooth. Stir in the sprinkles.
2. Microwave for about 1 minute. If the cake is not done, heat for an additional 15 seconds. Let the cake cool for a few minutes.
3. If using, top with a scoop of vanilla ice cream and decorate with rainbow sprinkles.

Oven and Air Fryer Instructions

1. Preheat the oven or air fryer to 350°F (175°C).
2. In an oversized oven-safe mug (or a greased 8-ounce/240-ml oven-safe ramekin or similar sized oven-safe baking dish), combine the flour, baking powder, sugar, milk, oil, and vanilla. Mix with a small whisk until the batter is smooth. Stir in the sprinkles.
3. If using the oven, bake for 20 to 30 minutes, until a toothpick inserted comes out clean. If using the air fryer, bake for 10 to 15 minutes, until a toothpick inserted comes out clean. Let the cake cool for a few minutes.
4. If using, top with a scoop of vanilla ice cream and decorate with rainbow sprinkles.

Hot Cocoa

This mug cake is flavored with hot cocoa mix and mini marshmallows, just like the hot chocolate from my childhood.

SERVES 1 OR 2

3 tablespoons all-purpose flour

1/4 teaspoon baking powder

2 teaspoons granulated sugar

1 tablespoon hot cocoa mix

3 tablespoons fat-free milk

1/2 tablespoon canola or avocado oil

5 mini marshmallows

Whipped Cream Frosting (page 183), for topping (optional)

Cocoa powder, for topping (optional)

Microwave Instructions

1. In an oversized microwave-safe mug, combine the flour, baking powder, sugar, hot cocoa mix, milk, and oil. Mix with a small whisk until the batter is smooth. Top with the mini marshmallows.
2. Microwave for about 1 minute. If the cake is not done, heat for an additional 15 seconds. Let the cake cool for a few minutes.
3. If using, top with the whipped cream frosting and a dusting of cocoa powder. This cake is best consumed while still warm or within a few hours of being cooked.

Oven and Air Fryer Instructions

1. Preheat the oven or air fryer to 350°F (175°C).
2. In an oversized oven-safe mug (or a greased 8-ounce/240-ml oven-safe ramekin or similar sized oven-safe baking dish), combine the flour, baking powder, sugar, hot cocoa mix, milk, and oil. Mix with a small whisk until the batter is smooth. Top with the mini marshmallows.
3. If using the oven, bake for 20 to 30 minutes, until a toothpick inserted comes out clean. If using the air fryer, bake for 10 to 15 minutes, until a toothpick inserted comes out clean. Let the cake cool for a few minutes.
4. If using, top with the whipped cream frosting and a dusting of cocoa powder. This cake is best consumed while still warm or within a few hours of being cooked.

Jell-O

This colorful cake tastes just like the gelatin dessert. You can experiment with all sorts of flavors and colors, just make sure not to use any sugar-free options. Kids will love this one too!

SERVES 1 OR 2

¼ cup (30 g) all-purpose flour

¼ teaspoon baking powder

1 teaspoon granulated sugar

3 tablespoons fat-free milk

½ tablespoon canola or avocado oil

1 tablespoon Jell-O gelatin powder

Whipped Cream Frosting (page 183), for topping (optional)

2 teaspoons rainbow sugar crystals, for topping (optional)

Microwave Instructions

1. In an oversized microwave-safe mug, combine the flour, baking powder, sugar, milk, oil, and gelatin powder. Mix with a small whisk until the batter is smooth.
2. Microwave for about 1 minute. If the cake is not done, heat for an additional 15 seconds. Let the cake cool for a few minutes.
3. If using, top with the whipped cream frosting and rainbow sugar crystals. Store any leftovers in the fridge or freezer in an airtight container.

Peanut Butter Cup

Growing up, my favorite Halloween candy was peanut butter cups. I still haven't really outgrown them. This cake replicates the coveted candy by sandwiching creamy peanut butter in the middle of a chocolate cake.

SERVES 1 OR 2

3 tablespoons all-purpose flour

¼ teaspoon baking powder

1 tablespoon granulated sugar

1 tablespoon unsweetened Dutch-process cocoa powder

3 tablespoons fat-free milk

½ tablespoon canola or avocado oil

1 tablespoon sweetened creamy peanut butter

Chocolate Ganache Frosting (page 182), for topping (optional)

Chocolate sprinkles, for decorating (optional)

Microwave Instructions

1. In an oversized microwave-safe mug, combine the flour, baking powder, sugar, cocoa powder, milk, and oil. Mix with a small whisk until the batter is smooth.
2. Gently place the peanut butter in the middle of the batter and press it down lightly until the cake batter just barely covers the peanut butter (see Note).
3. Microwave for about 1 minute. If the cake is not done, heat for an additional 15 seconds. Let cool completely.
4. If using, top with the chocolate ganache frosting and decorate with chocolate sprinkles. Store any leftovers in the fridge or freezer in an airtight container.

*Note

The peanut butter will sink during cooking, so you don't want to press it down too far or it will end up at the bottom.

Peanut Butter & Jelly

This starts with a peanut butter cake base, and the inside is filled with a jelly or jam surprise. (I prefer jam because of its thicker consistency.) Don't worry if your jelly/jam bubbles to the surface when the cake is cooking; it creates a nice lava effect.

SERVES 1 OR 2

¼ cup (30 g) all-purpose flour

¼ teaspoon baking powder

1 tablespoon plus 1 teaspoon granulated sugar

¼ cup (60 ml) fat-free milk

3 tablespoons sweetened creamy peanut butter

1 heaping tablespoon jelly or jam of choice

Microwave Instructions

1. In an oversized microwave-safe mug, combine the flour, baking powder, sugar, milk, and peanut butter. Mix with a small whisk until smooth. Using an ice-cream scoop, scoop out about half of the batter and set aside.
2. Drop the jelly or jam into the center of the mug, then top it with the remaining batter, making sure the jelly/jam is completely covered. Microwave for about 1 minute. If necessary, heat for an additional 15 seconds. Let cool completely. Store any leftovers in the fridge or freezer in an airtight container.

Oven and Air Fryer Instructions

1. Preheat the oven or air fryer to 350°F (175°C).
2. In an oversized oven-safe mug (or a greased 8-ounce/240-ml oven-safe ramekin or similar sized oven-safe baking dish), combine the flour, baking powder, sugar, milk, and peanut butter. Mix with a small whisk until smooth. Using an ice-cream scoop, scoop out about half of the batter and set aside.
3. Drop the jelly or jam into the center of the mug, then top it with the remaining batter, making sure the jelly/jam is completely covered. If using the oven, bake for 20 to 30 minutes, until a toothpick inserted comes out clean. If using the air fryer, bake for 10 to 15 minutes, until a toothpick inserted comes out clean. Let cool completely. Store any leftovers in the fridge or freezer in an airtight container.

S'mores

Ah, s'mores. The ultimate childhood snack experience. This recipe requires extra equipment if you want to achieve the roasted marshmallow effect since, unfortunately, a microwave can't give marshmallows that beautiful golden-brown tinge. Instead, you'll need either a kitchen torch or an oven to get the roasted look and texture. But if you love s'mores, it's worth the little bit of work.

SERVES 1 OR 2

¼ cup (24 g) ground graham cracker crumbs (about 1 sheet of graham crackers)

1 tablespoon melted unsalted butter

¼ cup (45 g) semisweet chocolate chips

3 tablespoons fat-free milk

2 tablespoons all-purpose flour

¼ teaspoon baking powder

½ tablespoon canola or avocado oil

1 large roasted or torched marshmallow, for topping (optional)

Microwave Instructions

1. In an oversized microwave-safe mug, combine the graham cracker crumbs and melted butter. Mix together until the crumbs are completely coated. Press down to form a crust evenly across the bottom of the mug.
2. In a small, microwave-safe bowl, combine the chocolate chips and milk. Microwave for 40 seconds and mix with a small whisk until the chocolate is completely melted. Add the flour, baking powder, and oil and mix with a small whisk until smooth. Transfer to the mug, on top of the graham cracker crust.
3. Microwave for about 1 minute. If necessary, heat for an additional 15 seconds. Let cool for a few minutes.
4. If using, top with a marshmallow. Store any leftovers in the fridge or freezer in an airtight container.

Timeless Snack Cakes

These old-fashioned cakes have been passed down for generations for a reason. They are so delicious to eat!

Blueberry Dump Cake

These cobbler-type cakes are typically made with premade pie filling and cake mix; mine uses frozen and fresh blueberries and, if you want, homemade cake mix. As the name suggests, everything is dumped into a pan and baked.

SERVES 6 TO 8

¾ cup (116 g) frozen blueberries

½ tablespoon cornstarch

3 tablespoons granulated sugar

½ cup (80 g) white cake mix, store-bought or homemade (see Note)

2 tablespoons unsalted butter, thinly sliced

¼ cup (38 g) fresh blueberries

Ice cream, for topping (optional)

Oven Instructions

1. Preheat the oven to 350°F (175°C). Grease an 8-inch (20 cm) square baking pan with nonstick cooking spray and line it with parchment paper.
2. Spread the frozen blueberries evenly across the pan. Sprinkle them with the cornstarch, then the sugar. Sprinkle the cake mix evenly across the pan, then top with the butter slices, distributing them evenly. Scatter the fresh blueberries on top.
3. Bake for about 30 minutes, then using a spatula or large spoon, push down any uncooked cake mix into the bubbling mixture. (Do not worry if this breaks the surface.) Continue baking for 15 to 20 minutes, until the surface is completely golden brown. Let cool for about 30 minutes.
4. If using, top with a scoop of your favorite ice cream. Store any leftovers in the fridge or freezer in an airtight container.

*Note

To make your own homemade white cake mix: In a large bowl, whisk together ½ cup (65 g) all-purpose flour, 1 teaspoon baking powder, ¼ cup plus 2 tablespoons (75 g) granulated sugar, 2 tablespoons nonfat dry milk powder, and 1 tablespoon cornstarch until well combined.

Vanilla

My vanilla cake is made without eggs, but it is every bit as moist and soft as classic vanilla cake.

SERVES 6 TO 8

1 cup (125 g) all-purpose flour

1½ teaspoons baking powder

¼ teaspoon salt

⅔ cup (119 g) granulated sugar

1 teaspoon vanilla extract or vanilla bean paste

2½ tablespoons melted unsalted butter

Whipped Cream Frosting (page 183), for topping (optional)

Oven and Air Fryer Instructions

1. Preheat the oven or air fryer to 350°F (175°C). Grease a 6-inch (15 cm) round baking pan with nonstick cooking spray and line the sides and bottom with parchment paper.

2. In a large bowl, whisk together the flour, baking powder, salt, and sugar until it looks light and powdery. Add the vanilla, melted butter, and ⅓ cup (80 ml) of water. Whisk until the batter is smooth and no lumps remain. (The batter will be very thick.) Add another ⅓ cup (80 ml) of water and whisk again until the batter is smooth. Transfer to the prepared baking pan.

3. If using the oven, bake for about 30 minutes, until a toothpick inserted comes out clean. If using the air fryer, bake for 10 to 15 minutes, until a toothpick inserted comes out clean. Let cool in the pan for 15 to 20 minutes, then transfer to a wire rack and let cool completely.

4. If using, top with the whipped cream frosting. Store any leftovers in the fridge or freezer in an airtight container.

Crazy Cake

Known as Crazy Cake or Depression Cake, this cake was created during the 1930s when resources like butter, milk, and eggs were scarce. This recipe may not include any of those ingredients, but it has a crumb that is just like classic cake. The classic recipe usually uses baking soda and vinegar, but my version uses baking powder instead.

Oven and Air Fryer Instructions

1. Preheat the oven or air fryer to 350°F (177°C). Grease a 6-inch (15 cm) round cake pan with nonstick cooking spray.
2. In a large bowl, whisk together the flour, baking powder, salt, cocoa powder, and sugar. Add the oil and water and whisk until the batter is smooth. Transfer to the prepared baking pan.
3. If using the oven, bake for 30 to 35 minutes, until a toothpick inserted comes out clean. If using the air fryer, bake for 12 to 18 minutes, until a toothpick inserted comes out clean. Let cool in the pan for 15 to 20 minutes, then transfer to a wire rack and let cool completely.
4. If using, top with the chocolate ganache frosting and decorate with chocolate curls or shavings. Store any leftovers in the fridge or freezer in an airtight container.

*Note

If you want to save some extra steps and dishes, skip the mixing bowl. The traditional way to make this cake is to mix all the ingredients directly in the pan. Just make sure to grease the pan first.

SERVES 6 TO 8

½ cup (63g) all-purpose flour

¾ teaspoon baking powder

⅛ teaspoon salt

2 tablespoons unsweetened Dutch-process cocoa powder

⅓ cup (67 g) granulated sugar

2 tablespoons canola or avocado oil

⅓ cup (80 ml) room temperature water

Chocolate Ganache Frosting (page 182), for topping (optional)

Chocolate curls or shavings, for decorating (optional)

French Yogurt

This soft, sweet, and slightly tangy cake is a classic that many children in France learn to make when they are young. For the traditional cake, you can use the glass yogurt container to measure out all the ingredients, which makes it easy for kids. I like to bake it in a regular cake pan, but you can also bake it as a loaf. Unlike the original, my version doesn't contain eggs, but it still comes out so soft and moist.

SERVES 6 TO 8

¾ cup (174 g) French-style vanilla yogurt (see Note)

3 tablespoons canola or avocado oil

½ cup (100 g) granulated sugar

1 cup (125 g) all-purpose flour

1½ teaspoons baking powder

¼ teaspoon salt

Oven and Air Fryer Instructions

1. Preheat the oven or air fryer to 350°F (175°C). Grease a 6-inch (15 cm) round cake pan with butter or nonstick cooking spray.
2. In a large bowl, whisk together the yogurt, oil, and sugar until evenly combined. Add the flour, baking powder, and salt and using a spatula, fold in until no lumps remain. Transfer to the prepared cake pan.
3. If using the oven, bake for 30 to 35 minutes, until lightly golden brown and a toothpick inserted comes out clean. If using the air fryer, bake for 12 to 18 minutes, until lightly golden brown and a toothpick inserted comes out clean. Let cool in the pan for 15 to 20 minutes, then transfer to a wire rack and let cool completely. Store any leftovers in the fridge or freezer in an airtight container.

✱Note

French-style yogurt is usually sold in small glass jars along with other yogurts in the dairy section of the grocery store. The yogurt is much thicker than regular yogurt, so don't substitute with regular yogurt. I prefer Oui brand.

Tomato Soup Cake

This is another unique cake from the Depression era, when resources were scarce. It uses canned tomato soup, which adds an umami flavor and a natural reddish hue I love. It isn't super sweet and is balanced with spices.

SERVES 6 TO 8

1 cup (125 g) all-purpose flour

1½ teaspoons baking powder

½ cup (100 g) granulated sugar

¼ teaspoon salt

½ teaspoon ground cinnamon

½ teaspoon ground nutmeg

Pinch ground cloves

¾ cup (180 ml) canned condensed tomato soup

2 tablespoons canola or avocado oil

Cream Cheese Frosting (page 183), for topping (optional)

Oven and Air Fryer Instructions

1. Preheat the oven or air fryer to 350°F (175°C). Grease a 6-inch (15 cm) round cake pan with nonstick cooking spray and line the bottom with a parchment round.
2. In a large bowl, whisk together the flour, baking powder, sugar, salt, cinnamon, nutmeg, cloves, tomato soup, and oil until the batter is smooth. Transfer to the prepared baking pan.
3. If using the oven, bake for about 30 minutes, or until a toothpick inserted comes out clean. If using the air fryer, bake for 12 to 18 minutes, until a toothpick inserted comes out clean. Let cool in the pan for 15 to 20 minutes, then transfer to a wire rack and let cool completely. Store any leftovers in the fridge or freezer in an airtight container.

21-and-Over Snack Cakes

Most of the cakes in this book are kid-friendly, but occasionally, we just need some "adult time." This chapter adds a little alcohol to the ingredient list. From a classy Champagne Cake (page 122) to a festive Margarita (page 118) to the über-decadent Kahlua Chocolate (page 117) and Chocolate Stout (page 114) cakes, these boozy treats are perfect to serve at parties—including parties of one.

Chocolate Stout

Stout beer has quite the bitter aftertaste, but when paired with chocolate, it adds another dimension to the cake and enhances the bittersweet notes of the chocolate. The result is one very enjoyable cake.

SERVES 1 OR 2

3 tablespoons all-purpose flour

¼ teaspoon baking powder

1 tablespoon granulated sugar

1 tablespoon unsweetened Dutch-process cocoa powder

2½ tablespoons fat-free milk

½ tablespoon canola or avocado oil

1 tablespoon stout beer

Whipped Cream Frosting (page 183), for topping (optional)

Chocolate syrup, for drizzling (optional)

Chocolate chips, for decorating (optional)

Microwave Instructions

1. In an oversized microwave-safe mug, combine the flour, baking powder, sugar, cocoa powder, milk, oil, and stout beer. Mix with a small whisk until the batter is smooth.
2. Microwave for about 1 minute. If the cake is not done, heat for an additional 15 seconds. Let the cake cool for a few minutes.
3. If using, top with the whipped cream frosting, a drizzle of chocolate syrup, and decorate with chocolate chips. Store any leftovers in the fridge or freezer in an airtight container.

Air Fryer Instructions

1. Preheat the air fryer to 350°F (175°C).
2. In an oversized oven-safe mug (or a greased 8-ounce/240-ml oven-safe ramekin or similar sized oven-safe baking dish), combine the flour, baking powder, sugar, cocoa powder, milk, oil, and stout beer. Mix with a small whisk until the batter is smooth.
3. Bake for 10 to 15 minutes, until a toothpick inserted comes out clean. Let the cake cool for a few minutes.
4. If using, top with the whipped cream frosting, a drizzle of chocolate syrup, and decorate with chocolate chips. Store any leftovers in the fridge or freezer in an airtight container.

Baileys Irish Cream

Take one whiff when this is finished cooking and you'll immediately detect the delightful Baileys Irish Cream. The sweet, creamy liqueur, so enjoyable on its own, is equally tasty when flavoring this cake.

SERVES 1 OR 2

¼ cup (30 g) all-purpose flour

¼ teaspoon baking powder

1 tablespoon granulated sugar

2 tablespoons fat-free milk

½ tablespoon canola or avocado oil

1 tablespoon Baileys Irish Cream

1 tablespoon bittersweet chocolate chips (see Note)

Microwave Instructions

1. In an oversized microwave-safe mug, combine the flour, baking powder, sugar, milk, oil, and Baileys. Mix with a small whisk until the batter is smooth. Stir in the chocolate chips.
2. Microwave for about 1 minute. If the cake is not done, heat for an additional 15 seconds. Let the cake cool for a few minutes. This cake is best consumed while still warm or within a few hours of being cooked.

Oven and Air Fryer Instructions

1. Preheat the oven or air fryer to 350°F (175°C).
2. In an oversized oven-safe mug (or a greased 8-ounce/240-ml oven-safe ramekin or similar sized oven-safe baking dish), combine the flour, baking powder, sugar, milk, oil, and Baileys. Mix with a small whisk until the batter is smooth. Stir in the chocolate chips.
3. If using the oven, bake for 20 to 30 minutes, until a toothpick inserted comes out clean. If using the air fryer, bake for 10 to 15 minutes, until a toothpick inserted comes out clean. This cake is best consumed while still warm or within a few hours of being cooked.

*Note

If you can get your hands on some cappuccino baking chips (found at specialty baking stores like King Arthur Flour), use those instead of chocolate chips for an even more intense creamy-coffee taste.

Kahlua Chocolate

Chocolate and coffee are a match made in heaven, so you can only imagine how marvelous this cake tastes with its chocolate base and a whisper of coffee liqueur.

SERVES 1 OR 2

3 tablespoons all-purpose flour

1/4 teaspoon baking powder

2 teaspoons granulated sugar

1 tablespoon unsweetened Dutch-process cocoa powder

2½ tablespoons fat-free milk

½ tablespoon canola or avocado oil

1 tablespoon Kahlua coffee liqueur

Microwave Instructions

1. In an oversized microwave-safe mug, combine the flour, baking powder, sugar, cocoa powder, milk, oil, and Kahlua. Mix with a small whisk until the batter is smooth.
2. Microwave for about 1 minute. If the cake is not done, heat for an additional 15 seconds. Let the cake cool for a few minutes. This cake is best consumed while still warm or within a few hours of being cooked.

Oven and Air Fryer Instructions

1. Preheat the oven or air fryer to 350°F (175°C).
2. In an oversized oven-safe mug (or a greased 8-ounce/240-ml oven-safe ramekin or similar sized oven-safe baking dish), combine the flour, baking powder, sugar, cocoa powder, milk, oil, and Kahlua. Mix with a small whisk until the batter is smooth.
3. If using the oven, bake for 20 to 30 minutes, until a toothpick inserted comes out clean. If using the air fryer, bake for 10 to 15 minutes, until a toothpick inserted comes out clean. This cake is best consumed while still warm or within a few hours of being cooked.

Margarita

This is another cake that's perfect for a party. You can even garnish the rim with some coarse sugar for the full effect!

SERVES 1 OR 2

¼ cup (30 g) all-purpose flour

¼ teaspoon baking powder

2 tablespoons granulated sugar

2 tablespoons fat-free milk

½ tablespoon canola or avocado oil

½ tablespoon tequila

1 teaspoon triple sec

¼ teaspoon lime zest

½ tablespoon fresh lime juice

Microwave Instructions

1. In an oversized microwave-safe mug, combine the flour, baking powder, sugar, milk, oil, tequila, triple sec, lime zest, and lime juice. Mix with a small whisk until the batter is smooth.

2. Microwave for about 1 minute. If the cake is not done, heat for an additional 15 seconds. Let the cake cool for a few minutes. Store any leftovers in the fridge or freezer in an airtight container.

Oven and Air Fryer Instructions

1. Preheat the oven or air fryer to 350°F (175°C).

2. In an oversized oven-safe mug (or a greased 8-ounce/240-ml oven-safe ramekin or similar sized oven-safe baking dish), combine the flour, baking powder, sugar, milk, oil, tequila, triple sec, lime zest, and lime juice. Mix with a small whisk until the batter is smooth.

3. If using the oven, bake for 20 to 30 minutes, until a toothpick inserted comes out clean. If using the air fryer, bake for 10 to 15 minutes, until a toothpick inserted comes out clean. Let the cake cool for a few minutes. Store any leftovers in the fridge or freezer in an airtight container.

Piña Colada

This cake will leave you dreaming of beaches and paradise. Inspired by the classic tropical cocktail, it's flavored with rum, pineapples, and coconut milk.

SERVES 1 OR 2

¼ cup (30 g) all-purpose flour

¼ teaspoon baking powder

2 tablespoons granulated sugar

½ tablespoon canola or avocado oil

3 tablespoons coconut milk

1 tablespoon dark rum

1 tablespoon diced canned pineapple

Cream Cheese Frosting (page 183), for topping (optional)

Pineapple syrup, for drizzling (optional)

Microwave Instructions

1. In an oversized microwave-safe mug, combine the flour, baking powder, sugar, oil, coconut milk, and rum. Mix with a small whisk until the batter is smooth. Stir in the pineapple.
2. Microwave for about 1 minute. If the cake is not done, heat for an additional 15 seconds. Let the cake cool for a few minutes.
3. If using, top with the cream cheese frosting and drizzle with pineapple syrup. Store any leftovers in the fridge or freezer in an airtight container.

Oven and Air Fryer Instructions

1. Preheat the oven or air fryer to 350°F (175°C).
2. In an oversized oven-safe mug (or a greased 8-ounce/240-ml oven-safe ramekin or similar sized oven-safe baking dish), combine the flour, baking powder, sugar, oil, coconut milk, and rum. Mix with a small whisk until the batter is smooth. Stir in the pineapple.
3. If using the oven, bake for 20 to 30 minutes, until a toothpick inserted comes out clean. If using the air fryer, bake for 10 to 15 minutes, until a toothpick inserted comes out clean. Let the cake cool for a few minutes.
4. If using, top with the cream cheese frosting and drizzle with pineapple syrup. Store any leftovers in the fridge or freezer in an airtight container.

Rum

This cake, scented with rum and vanilla, is quite pleasing on its own, but if you want the classic rum cake experience, don't skip the rum glaze.

SERVES 1 OR 2

Cake

¼ cup (30 g) all-purpose flour

¼ teaspoon baking powder

1½ tablespoons granulated sugar

3 tablespoons fat-free milk

½ tablespoon canola or avocado oil

½ teaspoon vanilla bean paste

1 tablespoon dark rum

Rum Glaze (see Note)

¼ cup (50 g) granulated sugar

1½ teaspoons dark rum

Microwave Instructions

1. To make the cake: In an oversized microwave-safe mug, combine the flour, baking powder, sugar, milk, oil, vanilla bean paste, and rum. Mix with a small whisk until the batter is smooth.
2. Microwave for about 1 minute. If the cake is not done, heat for an additional 15 seconds. Let cool while you prepare the rum glaze.
3. To make the rum glaze: In a microwave-safe mug or bowl, combine the sugar, rum, and ¼ cup (60 ml) of water and heat at 1-minute intervals, stopping to check in between, for 3 to 4 minutes, until it bubbles and thickens. Alternatively, you can cook the glaze in a small saucepan on the stovetop.
4. Using a toothpick or cake tester, poke holes all over the cake and immediately drizzle half of the glaze onto it before it cools and hardens. This cake is best consumed while still warm or within a few hours of being cooked.

*** Note**

This recipe makes enough rum glaze for two cakes.

Champagne

When you're in the mood to celebrate, this cake is perfect party fare. It leaves a lingering fizzy sensation on your tongue from the champagne bubbles. The champagne flavor is quite subtle, so I suggest enhancing it with a dollop of champagne frosting.

Microwave Instructions

1. To make the cake: In an oversized microwave-safe mug, combine the flour, baking powder, sugar, milk, oil, and champagne. Mix with a small whisk until the batter is smooth.
2. Microwave for about 1 minute. If the cake is not done, heat for an additional 15 seconds. Let cool for a few minutes.
3. Top with champagne frosting. This cake is best consumed while still warm or within a few hours of being cooked.

***Note**

If you'd like to turn things up a notch, add 2 to 3 drops of champagne extract to the batter, which will really enhance the flavor and effervescent notes of the champagne.

SERVES 1 OR 2

¼ cup (30 g) all-purpose flour

¼ teaspoon baking powder

1 tablespoon granulated sugar

2 tablespoons fat-free milk

½ tablespoon canola or avocado oil

2 tablespoons champagne

Champagne Frosting (page 185), for topping

Mimosa

Like the popular brunch drink, this cake is flavored with champagne and orange juice. Adding orange liqueur brings out the orange essence. It leaves a faint bubbly sensation on your tongue, and tastes even better with a dollop of champagne frosting!

SERVES 1 OR 2

¼ cup (30 g) all-purpose flour

¼ teaspoon baking powder

2 tablespoons granulated sugar

1 tablespoon fat-free milk

½ tablespoon canola or avocado oil

2 tablespoons champagne

½ tablespoon triple sec

1 tablespoon orange juice

Champagne Frosting (page 185), for topping

Silver sprinkles, for decorating (optional)

Microwave Instructions

1. In an oversized microwave-safe mug, combine the flour, baking powder, sugar, milk, oil, champagne, triple sec, and orange juice. Mix with a small whisk until the batter is smooth.

2. Microwave for about 1 minute. If the cake is not done, heat for an additional 15 seconds. Let cool for a few minutes.

3. Top with champagne frosting. If using, decorate with silver sprinkles. This cake is best consumed while still warm or within a few hours of being cooked.

Sweet Beer

While stout is more commonly used in desserts, this cake has a purer beer approach: light beer. You'll definitely taste the lingering yeast and hops in this sweet cake. Perfect for the beer lover with a sweet tooth.

SERVES 1 OR 2

¼ cup (30 g) all-purpose flour

¼ teaspoon baking powder

3 teaspoons granulated sugar

2 tablespoons fat-free milk

2 tablespoons light beer

Microwave Instructions

1. In an oversized microwave-safe mug, combine the flour, baking powder, sugar, milk, and beer. Mix with a small whisk until the batter is smooth.
2. Microwave for about 1 minute. If the cake is not done, heat for an additional 15 seconds. Let the cake cool for a few minutes. This cake is best consumed while still warm or within a few hours of being cooked.

Oven and Air Fryer Instructions

1. Preheat the oven or air fryer to 350°F (175°C).
2. In an oversized oven-safe mug (or a greased 8-ounce/240-ml oven-safe ramekin or similar sized oven-safe baking dish), combine the flour, baking powder, sugar, milk, and beer. Mix with a small whisk until the batter is smooth.
3. If using the oven, bake for 20 to 30 minutes, until a toothpick inserted comes out clean. If using the air fryer, bake for 10 to 15 minutes, until a toothpick inserted comes out clean. Let the cake cool for a few minutes. This cake is best consumed while still warm or within a few hours of being cooked.

Brownie Snack Cakes

As much as I enjoy my chocolate cakes, there is nothing that quite satisfies my chocolate cravings like a rich, decadent brownie. These brownies taste best if you give them time to cool completely to develop that chewy, dense, and fudgy texture. I know it's hard to have self-control when the brownie smells so mouthwatering after it's finished—but your patience will be rewarded.

Note: Most of the recipes in this section do require half of a large egg. I know this can be annoying to have leftover egg, but don't add the full egg, otherwise the texture just won't be the same. You can also double the recipe and make two brownies if you don't want to be left with part of an egg.

Dulce de Leche Brownie

The rich, salty-sweet dulce de leche, derived from the caramelization of sweetened milk (and literally translated as "candy of milk"), turns this already luscious brownie into a true indulgence. You'll be in a sugary heaven after just one bite.

SERVES 1 OR 2

1 tablespoon unsalted butter, plus more for greasing (optional)

2 tablespoons semisweet chocolate chips

1 tablespoon all-purpose flour

2 tablespoons beaten egg (½ large egg)

2 tablespoons dulce de leche, divided

Microwave Instructions

1. In an oversized microwave-safe mug, place the butter and chocolate chips. Microwave for about 40 seconds and mix with a small whisk until the chocolate is completely melted. Add the flour, beaten egg, and 1 tablespoon of the dulce de leche and whisk until the batter is smooth. Swirl in the remaining 1 tablespoon dulce de leche with a fork.
2. Microwave for about 1 minute. Let cool for about 30 minutes to set. Store any leftovers in the fridge or freezer in an airtight container.

Oven and Air Fryer Instructions

1. Preheat the oven or air fryer to 350°F (175°C).
2. In an oversized microwave-safe mug, place the butter and chocolate chips. Microwave for about 40 seconds and mix with a small whisk until the chocolate is completely melted. Add the flour, beaten egg, and 1 tablespoon dulce de leche and whisk until the batter is smooth. Swirl in the remaining dulce de leche with a fork.
3. If the mug is oven-safe, bake the cake in it. If not, transfer the batter to a greased 8-ounce (240 ml) oven-safe ramekin or similar sized oven-safe baking dish. Bake in the oven for 20 to 30 minutes, or in the air fryer for 10 to 15 minutes, until a toothpick inserted comes out clean. Let cool for about 1 hour to set. Store any leftovers in the fridge or freezer in an airtight container.

Lava Brownie

A rich, fudgy, chocolatey brownie with a gooey Nutella center? Yes, please! The silky hazelnut-chocolate filling makes for a blissful brownie experience.

SERVES 1 OR 2

1 tablespoon unsalted butter, plus more for greasing (optional)

2 tablespoons semisweet chocolate chips

1 tablespoon all-purpose flour

2 tablespoons granulated sugar

2 tablespoons beaten egg (½ large egg)

1 tablespoon Nutella

Whipped Cream Frosting (page 183), for topping (optional)

Chocolate shavings, for decorating (optional)

Microwave Instructions

1. In an oversized microwave-safe mug, microwave the butter and chocolate chips for about 40 seconds. Mix with a small whisk until the chocolate is completely melted. Add the flour, sugar, and beaten egg; whisk until smooth. Press the Nutella into the center of the batter, until completely covered. Microwave for about 1 minute. Let cool for a few minutes.
2. If using, top with the whipped cream frosting and decorate with chocolate shavings. This cake is best consumed while still warm (see Note). Store any leftovers in the fridge or freezer in an airtight container.

Oven and Air Fryer Instructions

1. Preheat the oven or air fryer to 350°F (175°C).
2. In an oversized microwave-safe mug, microwave the butter and chocolate chips for about 40 seconds. Mix with a small whisk until the chocolate is completely melted. Add the flour, sugar, and beaten egg; whisk until smooth. Press the Nutella into the center of the batter, until completely covered.
3. If the mug is oven-safe, bake the cake in it. If not, transfer the batter to a greased 8-ounce (240 ml) oven-safe ramekin or similar sized oven-safe baking dish. Bake in the oven for 20 to 30 minutes, or in the air fryer for 10 to 15 minutes, until a toothpick inserted comes out clean. Let cool for a few minutes.
4. If using, top with the whipped cream frosting and decorate with chocolate shavings. This cake is best consumed while still warm (see Note). Store any leftovers in the fridge or freezer in an airtight container.

* Note

This cake is best eaten while still warm but be careful because the Nutella lava center may still be very hot!

Cookies & Cream Blondie

This blondie is speckled with crushed Oreos. The crunchy chocolate-cookie crumbles add another layer of texture to these chewy and fudgy treats.

SERVES 1 OR 2

- 1 tablespoon unsalted butter, plus more for greasing (optional)
- 2 tablespoons all-purpose flour
- 2 tablespoons packed light brown sugar
- 2 teaspoons beaten egg
- 1 Oreo cookie

Microwave Instructions

1. In an oversized microwave-safe mug, microwave the butter for about 40 seconds, or until completely melted. Add the flour, brown sugar, and beaten egg. Mix with a small whisk until the batter is smooth. Add the Oreo and, using a fork, smash it into the batter until only small pieces remain.
2. Microwave for about 40 seconds. Let cool for about 30 minutes to set. Store any leftovers in the fridge or freezer in an airtight container.

Oven and Air Fryer Instructions

1. Preheat the oven or air fryer to 350°F (175°C).
2. In an oversized microwave-safe mug, microwave the butter for about 40 seconds, or until completely melted. Add the flour, brown sugar, and beaten egg. Mix with a small whisk until the batter is smooth. Add the Oreo and, using a fork, smash it into the batter until only small pieces remain.
3. If the mug is oven-safe, bake the cake in it. If not, transfer the batter to a greased 8-ounce (240 ml) oven-safe ramekin or similar sized oven-safe baking dish. If using the oven, bake for 20 to 30 minutes, until a toothpick inserted comes out clean. If using the air fryer, bake for 10 to 15 minutes, until a toothpick inserted comes out clean. Let cool for about 1 hour to set. Store any leftovers in the fridge or freezer in an airtight container.

Blondie

Dense and chewy, thick classic blondie cake is perfect on its own or as a base for any add-ins you like, such as butterscotch or chocolate chips, coconut flakes, chopped nuts, or dried cherries.

SERVES 1 OR 2

1 tablespoon unsalted butter, plus more for greasing (optional)

2 tablespoons all-purpose flour

2 tablespoons packed light brown sugar

2 teaspoons beaten egg

Microwave Instructions

1. In an oversized microwave-safe mug, microwave the butter for about 40 seconds, or until completely melted. Add the flour, brown sugar, and beaten egg. Mix with a small whisk until the batter is smooth.
2. Microwave for about 40 seconds. Let cool for about 30 minutes to set. Store any leftovers in the fridge or freezer in an airtight container.

Oven and Air Fryer Instructions

1. Preheat the oven or air fryer to 350°F (175°C).
2. In an oversized microwave-safe mug, microwave the butter for about 40 seconds, or until completely melted. Add the flour, brown sugar, and beaten egg. Mix with a small whisk until the batter is smooth.
3. If the mug is oven-safe, bake the cake in it. If not, transfer the batter to a greased 8-ounce (240 ml) oven-safe ramekin or similar sized oven-safe baking dish. If using the oven, bake for 20 to 30 minutes, until a toothpick inserted comes out clean. If using the air fryer, bake for 10 to 15 minutes, until a toothpick inserted comes out clean. Let cool for about 1 hour to set. Store any leftovers in the fridge or freezer in an airtight container.

Classic Chocolate Brownie

This is the quintessential brownie: fudgy, dense, chocolatey. I like to devour it plain, but if you prefer nuts in your brownies, go ahead and incorporate them—or add anything else you like.

SERVES 1 OR 2

- 1 tablespoon unsalted butter, plus more for greasing (optional)
- 2 tablespoons semisweet chocolate chips
- 1 tablespoon all-purpose flour
- 2 tablespoons granulated sugar
- 2 tablespoons beaten egg (½ large egg)

Microwave Instructions

1. In an oversized microwave-safe mug, place the butter and chocolate chips. Microwave for about 40 seconds. Mix with a small whisk until the chocolate is completely melted. Add the flour, sugar, and beaten egg and whisk until the batter is smooth.
2. Microwave for about 1 minute. Let cool for about 30 minutes to set. Store any leftovers in the fridge or freezer in an airtight container.

Oven and Air Fryer Instructions

1. Preheat the oven or air fryer to 350°F (175°C).
2. In an oversized microwave-safe mug, place the butter and chocolate chips. Microwave for about 40 seconds. Mix with a small whisk until the chocolate is completely melted. Add the flour, sugar, and beaten egg and whisk until the batter is smooth.
3. If the mug is oven-safe, bake the cake in it. If not, transfer the batter to a greased 8-ounce (240 ml) oven-safe ramekin or similar sized oven-safe baking dish. If using the oven, bake for 20 to 30 minutes, until a toothpick inserted comes out clean. If using the air fryer, bake for 10 to 15 minutes, until a toothpick inserted comes out clean. Let cool for about 1 hour to set. Store any leftovers in the fridge or freezer in an airtight container.

Nutella Brownie

If you enjoy the fudgy, chewy brownies you get with store-bought mixes, you are in luck. I've managed to recreate that texture with this recipe. And it's even easier to make than the box mix! Ultra chewy, fudgy, chocolatey, and sweet, this brownie is as good as it gets.

SERVES 1 OR 2

2 tablespoons all-purpose flour

2 tablespoons beaten egg (½ large egg)

¼ cup plus 1 tablespoon (92 g) Nutella

Microwave Instructions

1. In an oversized microwave-safe mug, combine the flour, beaten egg, and Nutella. Mix vigorously with a small whisk until completely incorporated. The batter will be quite thick.
2. Microwave for about 1 minute. Let cool for about 15 minutes to set. Store any leftovers in the fridge or freezer in an airtight container.

Oven and Air Fryer Instructions

1. Preheat the oven or air fryer to 350°F (175°C).
2. In an oversized oven-safe mug (or a greased 8-ounce/240-ml oven-safe ramekin or similar sized oven-safe baking dish), combine the flour, beaten egg, and Nutella. Mix vigorously with a small whisk until completely incorporated. The batter will be quite thick.
3. If using the oven, bake for 20 to 30 minutes, until a toothpick inserted comes out clean. If using the air fryer, bake for 10 to 15 minutes, until a toothpick inserted comes out clean. Let cool for about 1 hour to set. Store any leftovers in the fridge or freezer in an airtight container.

Spread Snack Cakes

I've already discussed my Nutella obsession and shared several luscious Nutella-based recipes in this book. But there are quite a few other equally delicious spreads out there that deserve some love, including peanut butter, cream cheese, and dulce de leche.

Peanut Butter

Creamy, moist, and rich: This is a dream cake for peanut butter fans. Make sure to use regular creamy peanut butter, rather than the kind with no added oils.

SERVES 1 OR 2

¼ cup (30 g) all-purpose flour

¼ teaspoon baking powder

1 tablespoon plus 1 teaspoon granulated sugar

¼ cup (60 ml) fat-free milk

3 tablespoons regular creamy peanut butter

1 scoop peanut brittle ice cream, for topping (optional)

Miniature milk chocolate chips, for decorating (optional)

Microwave Instructions

1. In an oversized microwave-safe mug, combine the flour, baking powder, sugar, milk, and peanut butter. Mix with a small whisk until the batter is smooth.
2. Microwave for about 1 minute. If the cake is not done, heat for an additional 15 seconds. Let the cake cool for a few minutes. If using, top with peanut brittle ice cream and miniature chocolate chips. This cake is best consumed while still warm or within a few hours of being cooked.

Oven and Air Fryer Instructions

1. Preheat the oven or air fryer to 350°F (175°C).
2. In an oversized oven-safe mug (or a greased 8-ounce/240-ml oven-safe ramekin or similar sized oven-safe baking dish), combine the flour, baking powder, sugar, milk, and peanut butter. Mix with a small whisk until the batter is smooth.
3. If using the oven, bake for 20 to 30 minutes, until a toothpick inserted comes out clean. If using the air fryer, bake for 10 to 15 minutes, until a toothpick inserted comes out clean. Let the cake cool for a few minutes. If using, top with peanut brittle ice cream and miniature chocolate chips. This cake is best consumed while still warm or within a few hours of being cooked.

Cheesecake

This cake needs to cool for several hours in the fridge to get the right texture. If you can't wait that long, you can eat it straightaway—it will still taste like a cheesecake but the texture won't be quite as dense and solidified.

SERVES 1 OR 2

1/4 cup (24 g) finely ground graham cracker crumbs

1 tablespoon unsalted butter, melted

1/4 cup (56 g) cream cheese spread (see Note)

2 tablespoons plain nonfat Greek yogurt

2 1/2 tablespoons granulated sugar

1 large egg, beaten

1/4 teaspoon vanilla extract

1/2 teaspoon freshly grated lime zest

Microwave Instructions

1. In an oversized microwave-safe mug, combine the graham cracker crumbs and melted butter. Mix together until the crumbs are completely coated. Press down to form a crust evenly across the bottom of the mug.
2. In a small bowl, combine the cream cheese spread, yogurt, sugar, egg, and vanilla. Mix vigorously with a small whisk until the batter is smooth. Transfer to the mug.
3. Cover the mug with a paper towel and microwave for 1 minute. The cake should be mostly cooked, except in the center. Heat for 20-second intervals, stopping to check in between, for about 1 minute, until the cake is completely cooked and pulling away from the mug. (You don't want to microwave for the full 2 minutes at once because the batter may overheat and start popping and exploding in the microwave.)
4. Gently slide the cheesecake out of the mug upside-down onto a large spatula and then flip it back over onto a plate. Let sit until cool enough to handle, then refrigerate for at least 1 hour, until completely cool and set.
5. Garnish with the lime zest. Store any leftovers in the fridge or freezer in an airtight container.

***Note**

Make sure to use cream cheese spread and not the block-style cream cheese. Cream cheese spread is smoother and easier to mix with a whisk.

Pumpkin Butter

Pumpkin butter used to be something I'd look forward to in the fall, but it's become so popular that it is now available year-round. This sweet spice spread adds a little something extra to the already moist and buttery cake.

SERVES 1 OR 2

1/4 cup (30 g) all-purpose flour

1/4 teaspoon baking powder

1 teaspoon granulated sugar

2 1/2 tablespoons fat-free milk

1/2 tablespoon canola or avocado oil

2 tablespoons pumpkin butter, divided

Microwave Instructions

1. In an oversized microwave-safe mug, combine the flour, baking powder, sugar, milk, oil, and 1 tablespoon of the pumpkin butter. Mix with a small whisk until the batter is smooth. Swirl in the remaining 1 tablespoon pumpkin butter with a fork. (Don't mix it in completely because you want to maintain gooey swirls of pumpkin butter.)

2. Microwave for about 1 minute. If the cake is not done, heat for an additional 15 seconds. Let the cake cool for a few minutes. This cake is best consumed while still warm or within a few hours of being cooked.

Oven and Air Fryer Instructions

1. Preheat the oven or air fryer to 350°F (175°C).

2. In an oversized oven-safe mug (or a greased 8-ounce/240-ml oven-safe ramekin or similar sized oven-safe baking dish), combine the flour, baking powder, sugar, milk, oil, and 1 tablespoon of the pumpkin butter. Mix with a small whisk until the batter is smooth. Swirl in the remaining 1 tablespoon pumpkin butter with a fork. (Don't mix it in completely because you want to maintain gooey swirls of pumpkin butter.)

3. If using the oven, bake for 20 to 30 minutes, until a toothpick inserted comes out clean. If using the air fryer, bake for 10 to 15 minutes, until a toothpick inserted comes out clean. Let the cake cool for a few minutes. This cake is best consumed while still warm or within a few hours of being cooked.

Dulce de Leche

This is one of my favorite mug cake recipes. Dulce de leche by itself is already out-of-this-world amazing. With gooey swirls throughout, each bite of cake is absolutely sublime.

SERVES 1 OR 2

1/4 cup (30 g) all-purpose flour

1/4 teaspoon baking powder

2 teaspoons granulated sugar

3 tablespoons fat-free milk

1/2 tablespoon canola or avocado oil

1 tablespoon dulce de leche, plus 1 tablespoon for topping (optional)

Whipped Cream Frosting (page 183), for topping (optional)

Chopped peanuts, for decorating (optional)

Microwave Instructions

1. In an oversized microwave-safe mug, combine the flour, baking powder, sugar, milk, and oil. Mix with a small whisk until smooth. Swirl in the dulce de leche with a fork until barely incorporated. (You want to maintain the gooey caramel swirls.)

2. Microwave for about 1 minute. If necessary, heat for an additional 15 seconds. Let cool for a few minutes (be careful with the hot dulce de leche).

3. If using, top with the whipped cream frosting, drizzle with the dulce de leche, and decorate with chopped nuts. This cake is best consumed while still warm or within a few hours of being cooked.

Oven and Air Fryer Instructions

1. Preheat the oven or air fryer to 350°F (175°C).

2. In an oversized oven-safe mug (or a greased 8-ounce/240-ml oven-safe ramekin or similar sized oven-safe baking dish), combine the flour, baking powder, sugar, milk, and oil. Mix with a small whisk until smooth. Swirl in the dulce de leche with a fork until barely incorporated. (You want to maintain the gooey caramel swirls.)

3. Bake in the oven for 20 to 30 minutes, or in the air fryer for 10 to 15 minutes, until a toothpick inserted comes out clean. Let cool for a few minutes (be careful with the hot dulce de leche).

4. If using, top with the whipped cream frosting, drizzle with the dulce de leche, and decorate with chopped nuts. This cake is best consumed while still warm or within a few hours of being cooked.

Almond Butter

This cake is flavored with a triple dose of almonds: almond butter, almond milk, and sliced almonds.

SERVES 1 OR 2

1/4 cup (30 g) all-purpose flour

1/4 teaspoon baking powder

2 tablespoons granulated sugar

2 tablespoons unsweetened almond butter

1/4 cup (60 ml) almond milk

4 or 5 sliced almonds

Microwave Instructions

1. In an oversized microwave-safe mug, combine the flour, baking powder, sugar, almond butter, and almond milk. Mix with a small whisk until the batter is smooth. Sprinkle the almonds on top.
2. Microwave for about 1 minute. If necessary, heat for an additional 15 seconds. Let cool for a few minutes. This cake is best consumed while still warm or within a few hours of being cooked.

Oven and Air Fryer Instructions

1. Preheat the oven or air fryer to 350°F (175°C).
2. In an oversized oven-safe mug (or a greased 8-ounce/240-ml oven-safe ramekin or similar sized oven-safe baking dish), combine the flour, baking powder, sugar, almond butter, and almond milk. Mix with a small whisk until the batter is smooth. Sprinkle the almonds on top.
3. Bake in the oven for 20 to 30 minutes, or in the air fryer for 10 to 15 minutes, until a toothpick inserted comes out clean. Let cool for a few minutes. This cake is best consumed while still warm or within a few hours of being cooked.

Holiday Snack Cakes

I love the variety of festive foods centered around holiday celebrations—from Valentine's Day chocolate through Christmastime eggnog. This chapter features enticing holiday-themed desserts that you can easily whip up for a special occasion, or any day of the year!

Guinness Chocolate–Irish Cream

Two popular alcoholic beverages that pop up during St. Patrick's Day are Guinness beer and Baileys Irish Cream. This cake combines them both into one extra-scrumptious snack.

SERVES 1 OR 2

3 tablespoons all-purpose flour

¼ teaspoon baking powder

2 tablespoons granulated sugar

1 tablespoon unsweetened Dutch-process cocoa powder

2 tablespoons fat-free milk

½ tablespoon canola or avocado oil

1 tablespoon Guinness beer

1 tablespoon Baileys Irish Cream

1 teaspoon confectioners' sugar, for topping (optional)

Microwave Instructions

1. In an oversized microwave-safe mug, combine the flour, baking powder, granulated sugar, cocoa powder, milk, oil, Guinness, and Baileys. Mix with a small whisk until smooth. Microwave for about 1 minute. If necessary, heat for an additional 15 seconds. Let cool for a few minutes.
2. If using, dust with the confectioners' sugar. This cake is best consumed while still warm or within a few hours of being cooked.

Oven and Air Fryer Instructions

1. Preheat the oven or air fryer to 350°F (175°C).
2. In an oversized oven-safe mug (or a greased 8-ounce/240-ml oven-safe ramekin or similar sized oven-safe baking dish), combine the flour, baking powder, granulated sugar, cocoa powder, milk, oil, Guinness, and Baileys. Mix with a small whisk until smooth.
3. If using the oven, bake for 20 to 30 minutes, until a toothpick inserted comes out clean. If using the air fryer, bake for 10 to 15 minutes, until a toothpick inserted comes out clean. Let cool for a few minutes.
4. If using, dust with the confectioners' sugar. This cake is best consumed while still warm or within a few hours of being cooked.

Chocolate Peppermint

Crushed peppermint candies give this chocolate cake a cool, minty finish to each bite.

SERVES 1 OR 2

- 1/4 cup (45 g) semisweet chocolate chips
- 3 tablespoons fat-free milk
- 3 tablespoons all-purpose flour
- 1/4 teaspoon baking powder
- 1/2 tablespoon canola or avocado oil
- 2 peppermint candies, finely crushed
- Whipped Cream Frosting (page 183), for topping (optional)

Microwave Instructions

1. In an oversized microwave-safe mug, microwave the chocolate chips and milk for about 40 seconds. Mix with a small whisk until the chocolate is completely melted. Add the flour, baking powder, and oil and whisk until smooth. Stir in the crushed peppermint candies.
2. Microwave for about 1 minute. If necessary, heat for an additional 15 seconds. Let cool for a few minutes.
3. If using, top with the whipped cream frosting. This cake is best consumed while still warm or within a few hours of being cooked.

Oven and Air Fryer Instructions

1. Preheat the oven or air fryer to 350°F (175°C).
2. In an oversized microwave-safe mug, microwave the chocolate chips and milk for about 40 seconds. Mix with a small whisk until the chocolate is completely melted. Add the flour, baking powder, and oil and whisk until smooth. Stir in the crushed peppermint candies.
3. If the mug is oven-safe, bake the cake in it. If not, transfer the batter to a greased 8-ounce (240 ml) oven-safe ramekin or similar sized oven-safe baking dish. If using the oven, bake for 20 to 30 minutes, until a toothpick inserted comes out clean. If using the air fryer, bake for 10 to 15 minutes, until a toothpick inserted comes out clean.
4. If using, top with the whipped cream frosting. This cake is best consumed while still warm or within a few hours of being cooked.

Easter Surprise

This simple white cake is studded with pastel sprinkles and has a melted mini Cadbury Creme Egg hidden in the center—because what's Easter without an egg hunt?

SERVES 1 OR 2

¼ cup (30 g) all-purpose flour

¼ teaspoon baking powder

2 teaspoons granulated sugar

3 tablespoons fat-free milk

½ tablespoon canola or avocado oil

¼ teaspoon vanilla extract

½ tablespoon pastel-colored sprinkles

1 mini Cadbury Creme Egg

Whipped Cream Frosting (page 183), for topping (optional)

Sprinkles, for decorating (optional)

Mini candy-coated chocolate eggs, for decorating (optional)

Microwave Instructions

1. In an oversized microwave-safe mug, combine the flour, baking powder, sugar, milk, oil, and vanilla. Mix with a small whisk until the batter is smooth. Stir in the sprinkles. Gently push the creme egg into the center of the batter until it is completely covered.
2. Microwave for about 1 minute. If the cake is not done, heat for an additional 15 seconds. Let the cake cool for a few minutes.
3. If using, top with the whipped cream frosting and decorate with sprinkles and mini candy-coated chocolate eggs. This cake is best consumed while still warm.

Oven and Air Fryer Instructions

1. Preheat the oven or air fryer to 350°F (175°C).
2. In an oversized oven-safe mug (or a greased 8-ounce/240-ml oven-safe ramekin or similar sized oven-safe baking dish), combine the flour, baking powder, sugar, milk, oil, and vanilla. Mix with a small whisk until the batter is smooth. Stir in the sprinkles. Gently push the creme egg into the center of the batter until it is completely covered.
3. If using the oven, bake for 20 to 30 minutes, until a toothpick inserted comes out clean. If using the air fryer, bake for 10 to 15 minutes, until a toothpick inserted comes out clean. Let the cake cool for a few minutes.
4. If using, top with the whipped cream frosting and decorate with sprinkles and mini candy-coated chocolate eggs. This cake is best consumed while still warm.

Gingerbread

This old-fashioned cake is spiced with molasses, cinnamon, and ground ginger. The taste is certain to evoke some wonderful winter memories.

SERVES 1 OR 2

¼ cup (30 g) all-purpose flour

¼ teaspoon baking powder

1 tablespoon packed dark brown sugar

¼ teaspoon ground ginger

⅛ teaspoon ground cinnamon

3 tablespoons fat-free milk

½ tablespoon canola or avocado oil

½ tablespoon dark molasses

Microwave Instructions

1. In an oversized microwave-safe mug, combine the flour, baking powder, brown sugar, ginger, cinnamon, milk, oil, and molasses. Mix with a small whisk until the batter is smooth.

2. Microwave for about 1 minute. If the cake is not done, heat for an additional 15 seconds. Let the cake cool for a few minutes. This cake is best consumed while still warm or within a few hours of being cooked.

Oven and Air Fryer Instructions

1. Preheat the oven or air fryer to 350°F (175°C).

2. In an oversized microwave-safe mug, combine the flour, baking powder, brown sugar, ginger, cinnamon, milk, oil, and molasses. Mix with a small whisk until the batter is smooth.

3. If the mug is oven-safe, bake the cake in it. If not, transfer the batter to a greased 8-ounce (240 ml) oven-safe ramekin or similar sized oven-safe baking dish. If using the oven, bake for 20 to 30 minutes, until a toothpick inserted comes out clean. If using the air fryer, bake for 10 to 15 minutes, until a toothpick inserted comes out clean. Let the cake cool for a few minutes. This cake is best consumed while still warm or within a few hours of being cooked.

Chocolate Halloween Candy

If you're looking for ways to use up leftover Halloween candy, check out this recipe: The chocolate cake base is made with plain chocolate bars, like Hershey's milk or dark chocolate, then it's studded with whatever chocolate candies the trick-or-treaters have left behind!

SERVES 1 OR 2

¼ cup (43 g) chopped plain milk or dark chocolate bars (such as Hershey's)

3 tablespoons fat-free milk

2 tablespoons all-purpose flour

¼ teaspoon baking powder

½ tablespoon canola or avocado oil

2 tablespoons chopped chocolate candies of choice (such as Snickers, Reese's, M&M's)

Microwave Instructions

1. In an oversized microwave-safe mug, combine the chopped chocolate and milk. Microwave for about 40 seconds. Mix with a small whisk until the chocolate is completely melted. Add the flour, baking powder, and oil and whisk until the batter is smooth. Stir in the chopped candy.
2. Microwave for about 1 minute. If the cake is not done, heat for an additional 15 seconds. Let the cake cool for a few minutes. This cake is best consumed while still warm or within a few hours of being cooked.

Oven and Air Fryer Instructions

1. Preheat the oven or air fryer to 350°F (175°C).
2. In an oversized microwave-safe mug, combine the chopped chocolate and milk. Microwave for about 40 seconds. Mix with a small whisk until the chocolate is completely melted. Add the flour, baking powder, and oil and whisk until the batter is smooth. Stir in the chopped candy.
3. If the mug is oven-safe, bake the cake in it. If not, transfer the batter to a greased 8-ounce (240 ml) oven-safe ramekin or similar sized oven-safe baking dish. If using the oven, bake for 20 to 30 minutes, until a toothpick inserted comes out clean. If using the air fryer, bake for 10 to 15 minutes, until a toothpick inserted comes out clean. Let the cake cool for a few minutes. This cake is best consumed while still warm or within a few hours of being cooked.

Pumpkin Spice

Throughout October and November, I'm obsessed with pumpkin everything! This is a spot-on single-serving version of one of my favorite fall treats.

SERVES 1 OR 2

¼ cup (30 g) all-purpose flour

¼ teaspoon baking powder

2 tablespoons granulated sugar

⅛ teaspoon ground cinnamon

⅛ teaspoon ground nutmeg

Pinch ground ginger

Pinch ground cloves

2 tablespoons fat-free milk

½ tablespoon canola or avocado oil

2 tablespoons pumpkin puree

Microwave Instructions

1. In an oversized microwave-safe mug, combine the flour, baking powder, sugar, cinnamon, nutmeg, ginger, cloves, milk, oil, and pumpkin puree. Mix with a small whisk until the batter is smooth.
2. Microwave for about 1 minute and 15 seconds. If the cake is not done, heat for an additional 15 seconds. Let the cake cool for a few minutes. This cake is best consumed while still warm or within a few hours of being cooked.

Oven and Air Fryer Instructions

1. Preheat the oven or air fryer to 350°F (175°C).
2. In an oversized oven-safe mug (or a greased 8-ounce/240-ml oven-safe ramekin or similar sized oven-safe baking dish), combine the flour, baking powder, sugar, cinnamon, nutmeg, ginger, cloves, milk, oil, and pumpkin puree. Mix with a small whisk until the batter is smooth.
3. If using the oven, bake for 20 to 30 minutes, until a toothpick inserted comes out clean. If using the air fryer, bake for 10 to 15 minutes, until a toothpick inserted comes out clean. Let the cake cool for a few minutes. This cake is best consumed while still warm or within a few hours of being cooked.

Eggnog

Surprise your loved ones on Christmas morning with this easy and delicious eggnog cake. It's nonalcoholic, so kids can enjoy this spice cake as well.

SERVES 1 OR 2

2 tablespoons cake flour (see Note)

1/8 teaspoon baking powder

3 teaspoons granulated sugar

3 tablespoons light eggnog

Microwave Instructions

1. In an oversized microwave-safe mug, combine the flour, baking powder, sugar, and eggnog. Mix with a small whisk until the batter is smooth.
2. Microwave for about 1 minute. If the cake is not done, heat for an additional 15 seconds. Let the cake cool for a few minutes. This cake is best consumed while still warm or within a few hours of being cooked.

Oven and Air Fryer Instructions

1. Preheat the oven or air fryer to 350°F (175°C).
2. In an oversized oven-safe mug (or a greased 8-ounce/240-ml oven-safe ramekin or similar sized oven-safe baking dish), combine the flour, baking powder, sugar, and eggnog. Mix with a small whisk until the batter is smooth.
3. If using the oven, bake for 20 to 30 minutes, until a toothpick inserted comes out clean. If using the air fryer, bake for 10 to 15 minutes, until a toothpick inserted comes out clean. Let the cake cool for a few minutes. This cake is best consumed while still warm or within a few hours of being cooked.

*Note

You must use cake flour to get the right texture; otherwise, it will have a much denser texture and will not taste like a cake.

Red Velvet

This cake is perfect for Valentine's Day, Christmas, or any other red-themed holidays. The recipe contains all the traditional ingredients found in red velvet, including buttermilk, baking soda, vinegar, and a touch of cocoa powder. Each one plays an integral role in the distinctive, hard-to-describe red velvet flavor and the puffy texture, as well as the pretty red color—which I tried to create without using copious amounts of food coloring.

SERVES 1 OR 2

¼ cup (30 g) all-purpose flour

⅛ teaspoon baking soda

2 tablespoons granulated sugar

½ tablespoon unsweetened Dutch-process cocoa powder, plus more for decorating (optional)

2 tablespoons buttermilk

½ tablespoon canola or avocado oil

⅛ teaspoon distilled white vinegar (see Note)

¼ teaspoon red food coloring, plus more as needed to reach desired color

Cream Cheese Frosting (page 183), for topping (optional)

Microwave Instructions

1. In an oversized microwave-safe mug, combine the flour, baking soda, sugar, cocoa powder, buttermilk, oil, vinegar, and food coloring. Mix with a small whisk until the batter is smooth.
2. Microwave for about 1 minute. If the cake is not done, heat for an additional 15 seconds. Let the cake for cool a few minutes.
3. If using, top with the cream cheese frosting and a dusting of cocoa powder. This cake is best consumed while still warm or within a few hours of being cooked.

Oven and Air Fryer Instructions

1. Preheat the oven or air fryer to 350°F (175°C).
2. In an oversized oven-safe mug (or a greased 8-ounce/240-ml oven-safe ramekin or similar sized oven-safe baking dish), combine the flour, baking soda, sugar, cocoa powder, buttermilk, oil, vinegar, and food coloring. Mix with a small whisk until the batter is smooth.
3. If using the oven, bake for 20 to 30 minutes, until a toothpick inserted comes out clean. If using the air fryer, bake for 10 to 15 minutes, until a toothpick inserted comes out clean.
4. If using, top with the cream cheese frosting and a dusting of cocoa powder. This cake is best consumed while still warm or within a few hours of being cooked.

*Note

Do not leave out any of the ingredients. People often try to omit the vinegar because they don't like the taste of it. But the vinegar is not added for taste; it interacts with the baking soda to make the cake fluffy and to help the cocoa powder develop the red hue.

Gluten-Free Snack Cakes

I receive a lot of requests for gluten-free recipes at Kirbie's Cravings, so I had to include a chapter of delicious gluten-free options. The best part about these is that you don't have to be living a gluten-free lifestyle to enjoy them. From the Almond-Chocolate Torte (page 162) to the Flourless Peanut Butter Cake (page 160) to the Chocolate Mochi Cake (page 159), you'll be tempted to try them all!

Flourless Chocolate

Unlike most recipes in this book, this cake needs to set for a few hours before you eat it—so plan ahead.

SERVES 1 OR 2

¼ cup (45 g) semisweet chocolate chips

1 tablespoon canola or avocado oil

1 large egg, beaten

Whipped Cream Frosting (page 183), for topping (optional)

Chocolate shavings, for decorating (optional)

***Note**

Because the mixture is so dark, it will be hard to see if egg streaks remain. Lift your whisk a couple times to make sure you don't see unmixed egg still in the batter.

Microwave Instructions

1. In an oversized microwave-safe mug, microwave the chocolate chips and oil for about 40 seconds. Mix with a small whisk until the chocolate is completely melted. Add the egg and whisk vigorously until the batter is smooth and the egg is fully incorporated (see Note). Microwave for about 1 minute, until the cake has risen and is set (it might look the slightest bit gooey on top). Let cool for several hours, so the chocolate flavor can fully develop.

2. If using, top with the whipped cream frosting and decorate with chocolate shavings. Store any leftovers in the fridge or freezer in an airtight container.

Oven and Air Fryer Instructions

1. Preheat the oven or air fryer to 350°F (175°C).

2. In an oversized microwave-safe mug, microwave the chocolate chips and oil for about 40 seconds. Mix with a small whisk until the chocolate is completely melted. Add the egg and whisk vigorously until the batter is smooth and the egg is fully incorporated (see Note).

3. If the mug is oven-safe, bake the cake in it. If not, transfer the batter to a greased 8-ounce (240 ml) oven-safe ramekin or similar sized oven-safe baking dish. If using the oven, bake for 20 to 30 minutes, until a toothpick inserted comes out clean. If using the air fryer, bake for 10 to 15 minutes, until a toothpick inserted comes out clean. Let cool for several hours, so the chocolate flavor can fully develop.

4. If using, top with the whipped cream frosting and decorate with chocolate shavings. Store any leftovers in the fridge or freezer in an airtight container.

Chocolate Mochi

Chocolate is not a typical mochi flavor, but it makes for a wonderful fusion of cultures. This East-meets-West cake is chocolatey and chewy, reminiscent of a brownie.

SERVES 1 OR 2

2 tablespoons glutinous rice flour (mochiko; see Note)

1/8 teaspoon baking powder

1 tablespoon granulated sugar

1/2 tablespoon unsweetened Dutch-process cocoa powder

2 tablespoons fat-free milk

1/2 tablespoon canola or avocado oil

Microwave Instructions

1. In an oversized microwave-safe mug, combine the glutinous rice flour, baking powder, sugar, cocoa powder, milk, and oil. Mix with a small whisk until the batter is smooth.

2. Microwave for about 1 minute. If the cake is not done, heat for an additional 15 seconds. Let the cake cool for a few minutes. This cake is best consumed while still warm or within a few hours of being cooked.

* Note

Despite what it sounds like, this "glutinous" rice flour is gluten-free. You can find it at most Asian grocery stores. It has also become more common in regular grocery stores in the US and through online retailers like Amazon. I use Koda Farms brand.

Flourless Peanut Butter

Unlike the other flourless cake recipes you'll find in this book, this one is not dense at all. It cooks up quite fluffy, almost like a regular peanut butter cake, and anyone eating it will be surprised that there is no trace of flour. Make sure to use regular peanut butter, rather than natural (with no added oils).

SERVES 1 OR 2

2 tablespoons regular creamy peanut butter

⅛ teaspoon baking powder

1 tablespoon granulated sugar

1 large egg

Vanilla ice cream, for topping (optional)

Caramel sauce, for drizzling (optional)

Chocolate chips, for decorating (optional)

Microwave Instructions

1. In an oversized microwave-safe mug, combine the peanut butter, baking powder, sugar, and egg. Mix vigorously with a small whisk until the batter is smooth and the egg is fully incorporated.
2. Microwave for about 1 minute. If the cake is not done, heat for an additional 15 seconds. Let cool for about 30 minutes so the peanut butter flavor can fully develop. If using, top with vanilla ice cream, drizzle with caramel sauce, and decorate with chocolate chips.

Oven and Air Fryer Instructions

1. Preheat the oven or air fryer to 350°F (175°C).
2. In an oversized oven-safe mug (or a greased 8-ounce/240-ml oven-safe ramekin or similar sized oven-safe baking dish), combine the peanut butter, baking powder, sugar, and egg. Mix vigorously with a small whisk until the batter is smooth and the egg is fully incorporated.
3. If using the oven, bake for 20 to 30 minutes, until a toothpick inserted comes out clean. If using the air fryer, bake for 10 to 15 minutes, until a toothpick inserted comes out clean. Let cool for about 30 minutes so the peanut butter flavor can fully develop. If using, top with vanilla ice cream, drizzle with caramel sauce, and decorate with chocolate chips.

Almond–Chocolate Torte

Made with almond flour, this cake is a lesson in chocolate indulgence: The absence of gluten makes the chocolate flavor all the more rich and intense.

SERVES 1 OR 2

3 tablespoons super-fine almond flour

¼ teaspoon baking powder

1 tablespoon granulated sugar

1 tablespoon unsweetened Dutch-process cocoa powder

2 tablespoons fat-free milk

Chocolate Ganache Frosting (page 182), for topping (optional)

Toasted flaked almonds, for decorating (optional)

Microwave Instructions

1. In an oversized microwave-safe mug, combine the almond flour, baking powder, sugar, cocoa powder, and milk. Mix with a small whisk until smooth.
2. Microwave for about 1 minute. If necessary, heat for an additional 15 seconds. Let cool for a few minutes.
3. If using, top with the chocolate ganache frosting and decorate with flaked almonds. This cake is best consumed while still warm or within a few hours of being cooked.

Oven and Air Fryer Instructions

1. Preheat the oven or air fryer to 350°F (175°C).
2. In an oversized oven-safe mug (or a greased 8-ounce/240-ml oven-safe ramekin or similar sized oven-safe baking dish), combine the almond flour, baking powder, sugar, cocoa powder, and milk. Mix with a small whisk until smooth.
3. If using the oven, bake for 15 to 20 minutes, until a toothpick inserted comes out clean. If using the air fryer, bake for 5 to 10 minutes, until a toothpick inserted comes out clean. Let cool for a few minutes.
4. If using, top with the chocolate ganache frosting and decorate with flaked almonds. This cake is best consumed while still warm or within a few hours of being cooked.

Peanut Butter–Banana

Bananas and peanut butter go hand in hand, but banana also gives this cake a denser texture, much like a classic flourless cake. For extra goodness, drizzle some caramel sauce on top.

SERVES 1 OR 2

1/4 teaspoon baking powder

1 tablespoon granulated sugar

2 tablespoons regular creamy peanut butter

2 tablespoons beaten egg (1/2 large egg)

2 tablespoons mashed overripe banana (about 1/2 large banana; see Note)

Ice cream, for topping (optional)

Caramel sauce, for topping (optional)

Microwave Instructions

1. In an oversized microwave-safe mug, combine the baking powder, sugar, peanut butter, beaten egg, and mashed banana. Mix with a small whisk until smooth. Microwave for about 1 minute. If necessary, heat for an additional 15 seconds. Let cool for a few minutes.
2. If using, top with the ice cream and caramel sauce. This cake is best consumed while still warm or within a few hours of being cooked.

Oven and Air Fryer Instructions

1. Preheat the oven or air fryer to 350°F (175°C).
2. In an oversized oven-safe mug (or a greased 8-ounce/240-ml oven-safe ramekin or similar sized oven-safe baking dish), combine the baking powder, sugar, peanut butter, beaten egg, and mashed banana. Mix with a small whisk until smooth.
3. If using the oven, bake for 20 to 30 minutes, until a toothpick inserted comes out clean. If using the air fryer, bake for 10 to 15 minutes, until a toothpick inserted comes out clean. Let cool for a few minutes.

3\. If using, top with the ice cream and caramel sauce. This cake is best consumed while still warm or within a few hours of being cooked.

*Note

The more overripe the banana, the easier it will be to whisk. Also, stay away from frozen bananas as they retain a great amount of water that will make the cake gummy.

Savory Snack Cakes

This section is devoted to savory cake-like creations—from Pizza Muffins (page 178) to Cornbread (page 176). For those times when you aren't craving a sweet snack, here's a stroll down the savory lane.

Crustless Quiche

This crustless quiche is so velvety and creamy. You can add just about any vegetable to it, and it makes for an easy brunch or breakfast dish.

SERVES 6 TO 8

3 large eggs

½ cup (120 ml) heavy cream

½ cup (36 g) shredded Cheddar cheese

½ cup (25 g) chopped vegetables, such as broccoli, asparagus, and spinach (see Note)

Oven Instructions

1. Preheat the oven to 350°F (175°C). Grease a 6-inch (15 cm) round baking dish with butter.
2. In a blender, blend the eggs and heavy cream until no egg streaks remain. (You can also use an immersion blender.)
3. Transfer the mixture to a large bowl. Stir in the cheese and vegetables. Transfer to the prepared baking dish.
4. Bake for 35 to 40 minutes, until fully cooked and not jiggly in the center. Let cool for a few minutes. This quiche is best consumed while still warm or within a few hours of being cooked. Store any leftovers in the fridge or freezer in an airtight container.

*Note

You can use any vegetables you like! Just try to avoid ones that will release a lot of water, such as squash, zucchini, and cauliflower.

Biscuit

This cake bakes up as a savory, flaky, soft biscuit. You can make it as one extra-large biscuit meant for sharing or make smaller individual biscuits. You can also easily customize it with mix-ins, or brush the top with honey for some sweetness.

SERVES 2 TO 4

½ cup plus 2 tablespoons (150 ml) heavy cream

1 cup (125 g) all-purpose flour

1½ teaspoons baking powder

½ teaspoon salt

Oven and Air Fryer Instructions

1. Preheat the oven to 425°F (215°C) or the air fryer to 400°F (200°C). Grease a 5-inch (12 cm) round baking dish with butter. (You can also use small individual oven-safe ramekins if you want to make individual biscuits rather than a big biscuit cake.)
2. In a large bowl, stir together the heavy cream, flour, baking powder, and salt until a wet dough forms and no flour streaks remain. Transfer the mixture to the prepared baking dish.
3. If using the oven, bake for 15 to 20 minutes, until golden brown and a toothpick inserted comes out clean. If using the air fryer, bake for 5 to 10 minutes, until golden brown and a toothpick inserted comes out clean. Let cool for a few minutes. This cake is best consumed while still warm or within a few hours of being cooked. Store any leftovers in the fridge or freezer in an airtight container.

Cheese Bread

This savory quick bread can be flavored with whatever cheese you prefer. You can even do a combination of different cheeses for more flavor. You can also double the recipe to make a larger loaf.

SERVES 6 TO 8

¾ cup plus 2 tablespoons (210 ml) seltzer water

1½ cups (180 g) all-purpose flour

2¼ teaspoons baking powder

½ teaspoon salt

½ cup (36 g) plus 1 tablespoon shredded Cheddar cheese (see Note), divided

Oven and Air Fryer Instructions

1. Preheat the oven to 375°F (190°C) or the air fryer to 350°F (175°C). Grease a 3 by 7-inch (7.5 by 17 cm) loaf pan with butter.
2. In a large bowl, stir together the seltzer water, flour, baking powder, and salt until a wet dough forms and no flour streaks remain. Stir in ½ cup (36 g) of the cheese until evenly incorporated. Transfer to the prepared loaf pan. Top with the remaining 1 tablespoon cheese.
3. If using the oven, bake for 30 to 35 minutes, until a toothpick inserted comes out clean. If using the air fryer, bake for 12 to 18 minutes, until a toothpick inserted comes out clean. Let cool completely. Store any leftovers in the fridge or freezer in an airtight container.

*** Note**

You can add other mix-ins in addition to the cheese, such as finely chopped cooked meats and herbs.

Pizza Bundt

This savory bundt cake is made up of pizza dough balls covered in tomato sauce and melted mozzarella cheese. You can slice and eat it like a cake, but it tastes like pizza.

SERVES 6 TO 8

1½ cups (188 g) all-purpose flour

2¼ teaspoons baking powder

½ teaspoon salt

1 cup (240 ml) plain nonfat Greek yogurt

1 cup (240 ml) marinara or pizza sauce, divided

1 cup (72 g) shredded mozzarella cheese, divided

Fresh basil leaves, for garnishing (optional)

***Note**

You don't want more than 2 layers of dough; otherwise, it's difficult for the dough at the bottom to cook through.

Oven Instructions

1. Preheat the oven to 350°F (175°C). Grease a 5-cup bundt pan with nonstick cooking spray.
2. In a large bowl, whisk together the flour, baking powder, and salt.
3. In a separate large bowl, add the yogurt and 1 cup (125 g) of the flour mixture. Mix until a sticky dough forms. Add more of the flour mixture as needed, until the dough is workable.
4. Scoop 1 tablespoon–size pieces of dough and roll them between your palms to form smooth balls.
5. Place 1 layer of dough balls in the prepared bundt pan. (The balls should be close together but not overlapping.) Top with ¼ cup (60 ml) of the marinara sauce, then ¼ cup (30 g) of the cheese. Place the remaining dough balls on top to create a second layer (you can tear some of them into smaller pieces to fill any gaps; see Note). Top with the remaining ¾ cup (180 ml) marinara sauce, spreading it evenly, and the remaining ¾ cup (80 g) mozzarella.
6. Bake for about 1 hour, or until a toothpick inserted comes out clean. Let cool for 15 to 20 minutes. Use a spatula to gently loosen the edges. Set a plate on top of the bundt pan and invert both to release the cake. If using, garnish with fresh basil leaves. This cake is best consumed while warm and the cheese is melted, but be careful it isn't too hot. Store any leftovers in the fridge or freezer in an airtight container.

Bacon Bread

This hearty, savory bread is soft and chewy, with bits of bacon mixed throughout. You can customize the bread further with other mix-ins as well!

SERVES 6 TO 8

- 1 cup (125 g) all-purpose flour
- 1½ teaspoons baking powder
- ¼ teaspoon salt
- ¾ cup (180 ml) plain whole milk yogurt
- ¼ cup (33 g) chopped cooked bacon

Oven and Air Fryer Instructions

1. Preheat the oven to 375°F (190°C) or the air fryer to 350°F (175°C). Grease a 3 by 7-inch (7.5 by 17 cm) loaf pan with butter.
2. In a large bowl, stir together the flour, baking powder, salt, and yogurt until all the flour is incorporated and a sticky dough forms. Stir in the bacon until evenly incorporated. Transfer to the prepared loaf pan.
3. If using the oven, bake for 20 to 25 minutes, until lightly browned and a toothpick inserted comes out clean. If using the air fryer, bake for 12 to 18 minutes, until lightly browned and a toothpick inserted comes out clean. Let cool for a few minutes. Store any leftovers in the fridge or freezer in an airtight container.

French Cake Salé

I don't think a savory cake section is complete without a recipe for cake salé, which is a classic French savory cake that has a texture like quick bread. The batter comes together in one bowl for easy preparation and can be filled with vegetables, meats, cheese, and more. This version I'm sharing adds pesto, sundried tomatoes (make sure to get the kind preserved in oil), and mozzarella cheese, but feel free to get creative with your mix-ins.

Oven Instructions

1. Preheat the oven to 350°F (175°C). Grease a 6-inch (15 cm) round cake pan with butter (see Note).

2. In a large bowl, whisk together the flour, baking powder, salt, eggs, milk, and oil until the batter is smooth. Stir in the mozzarella and sundried tomatoes until evenly incorporated. Add the pesto and swirl it throughout the batter a few times. (You do not need to fully mix in the pesto.) Transfer to the prepared baking pan.

3. Bake for about 30 to 35 minutes, until a toothpick inserted comes out clean. Let cool for a few minutes. This cake is best consumed while still warm or within a few hours of being cooked. Store any leftovers in the fridge or freezer in an airtight container.

✱Note

This cake is also often baked as a loaf cake, so you can bake it in a 3 by 7-inch (7.5 by 17 cm) loaf pan. The baking time will be about the same.

SERVES 6 TO 8

1 cup (125 g) all-purpose flour

1½ teaspoons baking powder

½ teaspoon salt

2 large eggs

¼ cup (60 ml) whole milk

3 tablespoons olive oil

½ cup (36 g) shredded mozzarella cheese (can substitute with other cheeses or cheese blends)

¼ cup (30 g) roughly chopped sundried tomatoes preserved in oil, lightly patted dry

2 tablespoons pesto sauce

Bacon Beer Muffin

Similar to a beer bread, but with a fluffier texture because it isn't baked for hours, this beer muffin carries a lingering trace of beer and bitter hops, balanced with savory smoky bacon.

SERVES 1 OR 2

¼ cup (30 g) all-purpose flour

¼ teaspoon baking powder

¼ teaspoon granulated sugar

3 tablespoons beer

½ tablespoon canola or avocado oil

1 tablespoon shredded Cheddar cheese

½ tablespoon chopped cooked bacon

Microwave Instructions

1. In an oversized microwave-safe mug, combine the flour, baking powder, sugar, beer, and oil. Mix with a small whisk until the batter is smooth. Stir in the cheese and bacon.

2. Microwave for about 1 minute. If the cake is not done, heat for an additional 15 seconds. Let the cake cool for a few minutes. This cake is best consumed while still warm or within a few hours of being cooked.

Cheddar Rosemary

Fragrant rosemary pairs perfectly with almost any cheese, especially sharp Cheddar. This fluffy cake is best eaten warm.

SERVES 1 OR 2

- 1/4 cup (30 g) all-purpose flour
- 1/4 teaspoon baking powder
- 1/8 teaspoon salt
- 1/4 cup (60 ml) fat-free milk
- 1/2 tablespoon canola or avocado oil
- 1/2 teaspoon chopped fresh rosemary
- 2 tablespoons shredded Cheddar cheese

Microwave Instructions

1. In an oversized microwave-safe mug, combine the flour, baking powder, salt, milk, and oil. Mix with a small whisk until the batter is smooth. Stir in the rosemary and cheese.
2. Microwave for about 1 minute. If the cake is not done, heat for an additional 15 seconds. Let the cake cool for a few minutes. This cake is best consumed while still warm.

Oven and Air Fryer Instructions

1. Preheat the oven or air fryer to 350°F (175°C).
2. In an oversized oven-safe mug (or a greased 8-ounce/240-ml oven-safe ramekin or similar sized oven-safe baking dish), combine the flour, baking powder, salt, milk, and oil. Mix with a small whisk until the batter is smooth. Stir in the rosemary and cheese.
3. If using the oven, bake for 20 to 30 minutes, until a toothpick inserted comes out clean. If using the air fryer, bake for 10 to 15 minutes, until a toothpick inserted comes out clean. Let the cake cool for a few minutes. This cake is best consumed while still warm.

Cornbread

This cornbread is unbelievably tender and moist—you may never want to make traditional cornbread again! It's perfect on its own or you can customize it however you wish. Sweeten it with honey, make it savory with bacon, or add spice with jalapeños. The possibilities are endless!

SERVES 1 OR 2

2 tablespoons all-purpose flour

2 tablespoons cornmeal

Pinch baking soda

½ tablespoon granulated sugar

2 tablespoons buttermilk

½ tablespoon canola or avocado oil

1 tablespoon beaten egg (¼ large egg)

Microwave Instructions

1. In an oversized microwave-safe mug, combine the flour, cornmeal, baking soda, sugar, buttermilk, oil, and egg. Mix with a small whisk until the batter is smooth.

2. Microwave for about 1 minute. If the cake is not done, heat for an additional 15 seconds. Let the cake cool for a few minutes. This cake is best consumed while still warm or within a few hours of being cooked.

Oven and Air Fryer Instructions

1. Preheat the oven or air fryer to 350°F (175°C).

2. In an oversized oven-safe mug (or a greased 8-ounce/240-ml oven-safe ramekin or similar sized oven-safe baking dish), combine the flour, cornmeal, baking soda, sugar, buttermilk, oil, and egg. Mix with a small whisk until the batter is smooth.

3. If using the oven, bake for 20 to 30 minutes, until a toothpick inserted comes out clean. If using the air fryer, bake for 10 to 15 minutes, until a toothpick inserted comes out clean. Let the cake cool before eating.

Pizza Muffin

One of the most popular recipes on Kirbie's Cravings are my pizza cupcakes. I adapted those cupcakes to make a single-serving muffin, and this one is pretty close in terms of taste and texture—and it comes out super cute.

SERVES 1 OR 2

¼ cup (30 g) all-purpose flour

⅛ teaspoon baking powder

⅛ teaspoon salt

1 teaspoon Italian seasoning, plus more for topping (optional)

¼ cup (60 ml) fat-free milk

½ tablespoon canola or avocado oil

2 tablespoons shredded mozzarella cheese, divided

14 mini pepperoni slices, divided

1 basil leaf, for garnishing (optional)

Marinara sauce, for serving

Microwave Instructions

1. In an oversized microwave-safe mug, combine the flour, baking powder, salt, Italian seasoning, milk, and oil. Mix with a small whisk until the batter is smooth. Stir in 1 tablespoon of the mozzarella and 7 of the mini pepperoni. If desired, transfer the batter to a 6-ounce (180 ml) microwave-safe ramekin for better presentation. Top with the remaining 1 tablespoon mozzarella and the remaining 7 pepperoni.
2. Microwave for about 1 minute. Let cool for a few minutes.
3. If using, top with a sprinkle of Italian seasoning and garnish with a basil leaf. Eat warm with a side of marinara sauce. Store any leftovers in the fridge or freezer in an airtight container.

Oven and Air Fryer Instructions

1. Preheat the oven or air fryer to 350°F (175°C).
2. In an oversized oven-safe mug, combine the flour, baking powder, salt, Italian seasoning, milk, and oil. Mix with a small whisk until the batter is smooth. Stir in 1 tablespoon of the mozzarella and 7 of the mini pepperoni. If desired, transfer the batter to a 6-ounce (180 ml) oven-safe ramekin for better presentation. Top with the remaining 1 tablespoon mozzarella and the remaining 7 pepperoni.
3. If using the oven, bake for 20 to 30 minutes, until a toothpick inserted comes out clean. If using the air fryer, bake for 10 to 15 minutes, until a toothpick inserted comes out clean. Let cool for a few minutes.
4. If using, top with a sprinkle of Italian seasoning and garnish with a basil leaf. Eat warm with a side of marinara sauce. Store any leftovers in the fridge or freezer in an airtight container.

Toppings

These are my go-to snack cake toppings. Just like the snack cake recipes, I kept the topping recipes simple. Feel free to add extra ingredients to elevate them even more. And of course, toppings are always optional. All the cakes in this book can be enjoyed as-is without anything extra.

Chocolate Ganache Frosting

MAKES ½ CUP (120 ML)

½ cup (90 g) semisweet chocolate chips

¼ cup (60 ml) heavy cream

1. Place the chocolate chips in a small heat-proof bowl.
2. In a small saucepan over medium heat, heat the heavy cream until simmering. Immediately remove it from the heat and pour it over the chocolate chips. Using a spatula, stir until the chocolate is completely melted and smooth.

Dairy-Free Chocolate Ganache Frosting

MAKES ½ CUP (120 ML)

½ cup (90 g) dairy-free dark chocolate chips

¼ cup (60 ml) canned coconut milk

1. Place the chocolate chips in a small heat-proof bowl.
2. In a small saucepan over medium heat, heat the coconut milk until simmering. Immediately remove it from the heat and pour it over the chocolate chips. Using a spatula, stir until the chocolate is completely melted and smooth.

Cream Cheese Frosting

MAKES ENOUGH FOR 2 INDIVIDUAL CAKES

2 tablespoons cream cheese, softened

2 tablespoons unsalted butter, softened

¼ cup plus 1 tablespoon (34 g) confectioners' sugar

1. In the bowl of a stand mixer fitted with the paddle attachment, or in a medium bowl using a handheld electric mixer, mix the cream cheese, butter, and confectioners' sugar at high speed until light and fluffy.

Whipped Cream Frosting

MAKES 1 CUP (240 ML)

½ cup (120 ml) heavy whipping cream

2 teaspoons granulated sugar

1. In the bowl of a stand mixer fitted with the whisk attachment, or in a large bowl using a handheld electric mixer, beat the heavy cream and sugar at high speed until peaks form.

Dairy-Free Whipped Cream Frosting

MAKES 1½ CUPS (360 ML)

1 can (13.66 ounces/403 ml) coconut cream, chilled in fridge for several hours or overnight

¼ cup (50 g) granulated sugar

1. Open the can of chilled coconut cream and scoop out only the solid white part. Transfer to the bowl of a stand mixer fitted with the whisk attachment and add the sugar.
2. Beat at high speed until the mixture is thick and has the consistency of whipped cream. (If your cream is a little grainy, you may need to add a small amount of the liquid from the can until you have a light and fluffy frosting.)

Streusel Topping

MAKES 3 TABLESPOONS

½ tablespoon cold unsalted butter, chopped into tiny pieces

¾ tablespoon all-purpose flour

1 tablespoon plus 1 teaspoon packed light brown sugar

Pinch ground cinnamon

1. In a small bowl, combine the butter, flour, brown sugar, and cinnamon until evenly incorporated.

Champagne Frosting

MAKES ENOUGH FOR 2 INDIVIDUAL CAKES

½ cup (120 ml) heavy whipping cream

1 tablespoon champagne

2 teaspoons granulated sugar

1. In a small bowl, combine the heavy cream, champagne, and sugar and using an electric hand mixer, beat at high speed until peaks form.

Vanilla Glaze

MAKES 3 TABLESPOONS

½ cup (54 g) confectioners' sugar

½ teaspoon vanilla extract

1. In a small bowl, whisk together the confectioners' sugar, vanilla extract, and 1½ teaspoons of water until smooth. If you prefer a thinner glaze, add water, ¼ teaspoon at a time, to reach your desired consistency.

Index

D

E

Acknowledgments

Being an author has always been my dream. As a child, I spent countless hours in the library, and I spent nearly all my free time reading books. While this isn't my first book to be published, it is still such a surreal feeling to be given the opportunity to write this book.

This book wouldn't be possible without the help of many others.

To Rage, thank you for liking my first cookbook enough to want to come out with this new edition. I would not have had this opportunity again without your help. To Kristy and Erin, thank you for all your help editing this book. Thank you to all the rest of the Quarto Publishing Group members that worked on this book.

Thank you to all my readers. I wouldn't have a website or my books without you. Thank you for giving me the motivation to continue to create new recipe ideas every day. Hearing your positive feedback and experiences after making my recipes is always a highlight of my day.

Thank you to my family. My parents, for always believing in me, supporting me, and teaching me to work hard. My siblings, for their support and for being my go-to taste testers. To my husband and son, for being patient while I stressed over writing this book, happily tasting every version of every recipe, and helping with the massive clean-up.

To Sarah, who donated her time to someone she barely knew and helped me with my first book proposal. She started me on this journey and I'm forever grateful for that.

About the Author

Jennifer Lee is a cookbook author and creator of the popular food blog, *Kirbie's Cravings*, a website that shares thousands of easy recipes with minimal ingredients. Her website receives millions of views each month and her recipes have been featured in numerous publications, including *People*, *Cosmopolitan*, *SELF*, *Country Living*, and more.

Jennifer loves food and spends most of her time thinking about food. She has always enjoyed baking for others. She also has a serious sweet tooth and believes that there is a separate stomach for dessert. When she's not in the kitchen, she likes to travel to places to eat and taste more food.